P9-DBO-613

Christopher Holliday
photographs by Jerry Harpur

Sharp
GARDENING

Sharp
GARDENING

Christopher Holliday
photographs by Jerry Harpur

TIMBER PRESS
Portland, Oregon

To my parents and David

Sharp Gardening
Copyright © Frances Lincoln Ltd 2005
Text copyright © Christopher Holliday 2005
Illustrations copyright © Jerry Harpur 2005

First published in North America in 2005 by
Timber Press, Inc.
The Haseltine Building
133 S.W. Second Avenue, Suite 450
Portland, Oregon 97204-3527, U.S.A.
www.timberpress.com

All rights reserved.
No part of this publication may be reproduced, stored in a
retrieval system, or transmitted, in any form, or by any means,
electronic, mechanical, photocopying, recording or otherwise
without either prior permission in writing from the publisher
or a licence permitting restricted copying.

A catalog record for this book is available from
the Library of Congress

ISBN 0-88192-699-x

Printed and bound by KHL Printing Co. in Singapore

2 4 6 8 9 7 5 3 1

Page 1: Echinops.
Pages 2–3: *Elymus magellanicus*.
Opposite: The rhinoceros horn leaf of *Agave americana*.

CONTENTS

A desert-style planting in Montecito, California, that portrays the vertical silhouettes and rigid outlines of the sharp gardening look.

Introduction

What is sharp gardening?

'Sharp gardening?' you may be asking. 'What on earth is that?' It is a new style of gardening that has emerged in response to contemporary lifestyles and opportunities.

There was once a time when a garden was designed to create pleasant areas where ladies and gentlemen might sit or stroll, and to provide fresh flowers for the house and fruit and vegetables for the table, all tended by dozens of gardeners. Even though those labour-intensive days may be long gone, many still dream of a romantic cottage garden full of flowers and perhaps vegetables, while for others a traditional layout with a lawn and herbaceous borders remains the priority. But these styles of gardening guzzle time too. Borders planted predominantly with flowering perennials produce best results when the plants are mulched and fed, staked as necessary, cut back in autumn and divided every few seasons. Lawns are notoriously high maintenance, requiring feeding, weeding, moss-killing, aerating, mowing and watering. Today paid help does not come cheaply; and with more demands on time, for most people the hours available to indulge in gardening have somehow become fewer. Gardening is now a DIY pastime, enjoyed in hours snatched at weekends and the odd evening.

Not only is time finite. Today's gardens, especially those of new housing plots, are smaller than they were in the past, so there is less space to garden in. Space counts more than ever before and every plant has to earn its keep.

At the same time there is a growing recognition that a satisfying design does not have to depend on flower colour alone, and that textures of foliage are just as fulfilling. Although structure provided by plants is always useful, gardens do not necessarily require labour-intensive topiary or over-familiar evergreen shrubs to achieve it. Nor does colour have to come from time-consuming herbaceous borders. In addition to these ideas, gardeners now have a more diverse selection of plants available to them than ever before.

Gardeners can capitalize on all these developments in a way that suits the twenty-first-century lifestyle by sharp gardening. This is a different kind of gardening, which guarantees:

- massive impact, however small the plot
- an even spread of interest throughout the year
- tolerance of dry conditions
- structure relying on planting rather than hard landscaping
- an exciting look, using an exotic type of planting
- low-maintenance planting without a lawn.

THE SHARP PALETTE

Sharp gardening is based on the use of spiky, sword-leaved plants, many of them evergreen, including large specimen exotics with an architectural profile. These are complemented by low-maintenance perennials with flowers or foliage that echo or contrast with the forms of the larger structural plants; and ornamental grasses complete the look with their contrasting forms and bristle-sharp pointed tips. Architectural plants are key. But a solitary New Zealand cabbage palm, *Cordyline australis*, embedded in the front lawn is not enough: sharp gardening relies on growing these specimens *en masse* to create a unified design.

By using only plants that pay their way, this style casts off the romantic and nostalgic traditions of the twentieth century. You won't have the luxury of blooms of great but transient beauty such as magnolias and peonies. By selecting from the rich pool of architectural evergreens available and a strict palette of perennials and grasses, replacing those roses and clematis with, say, yuccas, thistles and stipas, you can establish a garden that has an even spread of interest throughout the year. A permanent charismatic presence of evergreen architectural plants, providing more to look at than the earth and bare stems of a traditional herbaceous border, makes the long haul through winter feel less arduous. And with its crisp, clean style, sharp gardening makes a dramatic impact. Even in small, urban gardens larger-than-life plants do not look out of place and create a cohesive design; indeed, since many of the plants have a vertical habit this style lends itself to a small area.

In this book I divide the architectural plants into two groups: those I describe as swords and lances, discussed in the chapter beginning on page 28, and spiky rosettes, discussed in the chapter beginning on page 76. Many of the swords and lances are subtropical in appearance but able to withstand temperate climates. Most require good drainage and are better able to shrug off temperatures below freezing if kept dry in winter. Plants from South Africa, Mexico, Australia, New Zealand and South America form the backbone of this style. These plants are low maintenance because they are not rich feeders and do not require mollycoddling in the form of staking or need excessive cutting back.

Amongst the spiky rosettes there are plants that have adapted themselves to withstand

Californian Zen: Octopus-like *Agave americana* with a grey-leaved crassula to the left, on poured concrete terraces at Carol Valentine's garden in Montecito, California, designed by Isabelle Greene.

extreme temperatures and drought. These plants are originally from hot, arid regions and used to searingly hot temperatures with little rainfall. Some are succulents that store moisture in their swollen leaves and stems. Others have leaves with waxy surfaces and fine hairs that reduce loss of water by transpiration, or silver and grey leaves that reflect sunlight. Or they are low-growing plants with small leaves that are less prone to losing moisture through transpiration. These drought-tolerant qualities are in tune with an age that recognizes that resources are not inexhaustible and requires a water-wise attitude, and they free the gardener from time-consuming watering. Grasses are practical perennials for exposed sites and open sunny gardens, and low maintenance too.

A few other plants embroider the look with their paddle-shaped pointed leaves and exotic flowers: cannas, hedychiums and others, which spice up the planting. These enjoy the good life; they thrive on damper ground and are rich feeders.

This approach is inspired by the subtropical gardens of the past, which have been reinvented for the modern garden. Enthusiasm for spiky plants erupted in the days of the great nineteenth-century plant-hunting expeditions, when the bold foliage of palms, in particular, creating the impression of warmth, blue skies and sparkling light, beguiled the inhabitants of northern Europe. The British were thrilled to grow palms and other exotics on the French Riviera, while back home Victorians could not resist assembling confections of subtropical foliage, jostling bedding schemes of cannas around palm trees. In the appropriate hardiness zones of the United States subtropical plants were imported to line avenues and punctuate backyards.

There is nothing quite as exotic as a palm – they make excellent focal points, piercing the sky with their jagged outlines and establishing a unique look. But the spectrum of spikes, swords and lances is immense, and gardeners who do not choose these sharp plants and mass them together miss out on their potency.

THE SHARP PICTURE

Well-designed gardens owe their success to contrasting shapes and sizes and this is no less true in the case of the sharp garden. At the simplest level, good foils depend on juxtaposing verticals with horizontals and hard with soft forms. In a sharp garden with a strong backbone of swords and spikes, contrasts can often be sought from the spikes themselves: some spiky leaves grow as rosettes either on the ground or on each stem, their rounded shapes offering a breather from spear-like foliage. Then, by adding perennials and grasses, like an artist painting in the details, you can gain a contrast between these and the dagger silhouettes that form the backbone of the design.

But no matter how much you chase after perfect partnerships of forms and textures, much of the fun still comes from growing flowers. If the rigid forms of key foliage plants make up the evergreen skeleton of the design, flowering perennials with appropriate-looking blooms flesh it out and turn a selection of swords and spears into a cohesive design. I discuss these in the chapter beginning on page 116. Barbed thistles covered in spines are natural choices. The thrusting spires of

A parade of variegated *Cordyline australis* 'Albertii' with *Agave americana* (right) and *Dasylirion achrotrichum* (centre) at the Abbey Gardens, Tresco.

plants such as kniphofias and eremurus echo the tall spikes of inflorescences that erupt from desert succulents such as agaves. Globe flowers accompanied by strappy leaves that echo pointed foliage alter the tempo of a design. The drumstick heads of alliums and agapanthus are a case in point: their spherical blooms contrast with angular leaves, while their strap leaves echo lance-shaped foliage.

While spiky plants explode, feathery grasses float. Harnessed, they offer infinite tactile combinations, and their shapes are elegant for much of the year. Quivering foliage and seedheads seem to emerge like fountains among the vertical accents of spiky flowers. Successful alliances between individual plants develop into stimulating planting schemes. I develop these ideas in the final chapter beginning on page 160.

Sharp gardening involves discipline, because the greatest effects are produced by not being a plantaholic; repeating key plants rather than amassing many different kinds of plant creates a much stronger design. It also demands focus: gardeners must not allow themselves to deviate from the theme with plants that look out of place or are unsuited to the growing conditions.

CREATING THE SHARP LOOK

I hit upon the exotic style of planting in my garden unwittingly. My first garden, overlooking the tidal estuary of Morecambe Bay in Cumbria, has a steep hillside location, with free-draining stony soil above porous limestone. Mild coastal winters supply the necessary conditions for frost-hardy plants such as bold, thrusting phormiums. In an area noted for its grey days I felt I needed evergreens with a presence, and I could not resist planting entire borders with phormiums, especially those with red, cream or golden variegations. In doing so I established a seaside garden that looked comfortable with the surroundings. I was hooked.

By studying plants that constitute a subtropical theme, many of which are described and illustrated in this book, you can choose your own sharp favourites; and by absorbing sharp designs made in ideal growing conditions you can decide on the particular effect you wish to achieve. Choose what's best for you from the gardens illustrated that strike a chord with you. If a garden makes your heart sing, why not attempt to recreate its best attributes for your own style of planting?

To grow your chosen plants successfully, grasping their preferred growing conditions is vital. To do this, you need to be aware of their hardiness. A plant's survival depends on its hardiness, denoted by whether it is frost tender, half hardy, frost hardy or fully hardy.

Frost tender	liable to be damaged by temperatures below 5°C/41°F
Half hardy	withstands temperatures down to 0°C/32°F
Frost hardy	withstands temperatures down to −5°C/23°F
Fully hardy	withstands temperatures down to −15°C/5°F

These descriptions are only a rough guide to a plant's ability to withstand extremes of cold. If the roots are dry a frost will not be as harmful as it will be if they are wet, as dry roots will not freeze so readily. Although a plant's hardiness is indicated in gardening encyclopaedias, it is often a case of trial and error in your garden to see what you can safely get away with. This is the essence of gardening for many – the endless fascination of what you can and cannot grow. If you are a beginner, it is important to discover which plants your climate can support, and select plants appropriately.

Since plants from arid areas of the globe can withstand temperatures below freezing only if kept dry, where rainfall is high in the winter months – which in a temperate climate it normally is – a combination of wet and cold can be disastrous. Too much rainfall and frost reduces some barbed spears to mush. The odd night of frost in dry conditions may not do too much damage, unless the plant is half hardy or frost tender. But more often than not, it is prolonged wet weather followed by a burst of frost that deals the hardest blow.

Although many of these plants like plenty of moisture, they cannot bear sitting in it. Well-drained soil is key. Most gardens in a temperate climate will be much wetter than the plants require, which is why drainage is so important. Most of them also prefer a sunny spot, although some will take partial shade. If you are gardening in an undrained frost pocket, in deep shade or on leaden clay soil, be wary of pursuing sharp gardening! However, if you are without or can improve on these problems, the possibilities for enjoyment are endless.

Such plants' survival depends not only on their hardiness, exposure to recent rainfall and adequate drainage but also on the movement of air around them. The more air around a plant, and the drier the soil, the better.

Although sharp gardening leans heavily on plants from the southern hemisphere, many of which are frost hardy or half hardy, it is possible to achieve the look if you select those that will flourish in the cooler and wetter northern hemisphere. If you dig deep you will discover a wealth of frost-hardy and half-hardy plants that will do the job more than happily. Although cooler than urban or seaside locations, inland gardens in the UK are able to support many frost-hardy or half-hardy trees, shrubs and perennials. If you are an urban gardener, you are likely to enjoy the benefits of a city microclimate; there are often microclimate areas in other gardens too. And as in Britain we get more daring after a succession of warmer winters, the sharp gardener can let rip by trying to

ABOVE A *Trachycarpus fortunei* frames the view of this intimate corner in Brighton, Sussex.

grow plants that twenty or thirty years ago even gardening experts were much more cautious about cultivating. Hotter summers ripen the wood on plants and help them to withstand cold winters. Together with increased availability of unusual plants, a warmer climate has expanded the possibilities for exciting schemes. The plants are there. It's up to you to try them out and put them together.

To grow these plants successfully in wetter, but not necessarily cooler, regions the gardener has to replicate their preferred growing conditions.

- The most obvious way is to grow them in the most free-draining conditions possible. Add grit when planting to improve drainage. Incorporate raised beds into your design, as these ensure that rainfall runs through the soil quickly and never becomes waterlogged.
- It helps the tenderest plants to be placed at the highest level, as cold air drains away from the highest point more easily and thoroughly.
- Mulch with pebbles or stones, so that the neck of the plant is kept drier, which helps to prevent the plant from rotting.
- Many of the most tender plants described in this book require an open situation, but a location on the south side of a tree may be better than an open situation as it will be drier and the tree canopy will keep the rain off the ground too. Likewise an overhanging roof or porch will offer protection.
- Even different areas of your garden will provide better conditions than others. Borders by south- or west-facing house or garden walls will be more protected from frost.
- Wrapping a plant in fleece when frost is expected will benefit the plant. If you have nothing to hand, and the forecast is grim, throw a towel or old sheet over it.
- For prized frost-tender and half-hardy specimens, there may be no alternative but to grow the plant as a containerized specimen, which can be brought under cover in winter.

TOP Spiky rosettes and spires of bottle brush *Yucca filifera*.
BOTTOM Cushions of golden barrel cactus (*Echinocactus grusonii*), which can be copied with bun-shaped subshrubs in temperate zones, make good contrasts for lance-leaved plants in a sharp design.

In temperate gardens, it may be impossible to create the perfect growing conditions for some exotic plants: it will be too wet or too cold. What you can try to achieve is the look. By looking at, say, gardens in Mexico filled with exotic succulents you can pick out shapes you wish to echo and copy them with suitable plants in your own garden. If a favourite plant does not grow in your climate, there is likely to be a look-alike that will.

By choosing the right plants and giving them the appropriate growing conditions, the sharp garden look is yours for the asking. You won't get it right first time, but you should have a lot of fun exploring possibilities. I have been trying to grow the tricky biennial *Echium pinnato* for a decade and have only had two good years, but I remain optimistic. I have been drawn to this style of gardening because it looks good and is easy and low maintenance – I see no point in spending precious summer hours spraying and staking when I could be sitting under a palm tree reading. I have been influenced by visiting gardens abroad, and the photographs in *Sharp Gardening* reveal the ultimate spiky planting schemes in some of the finest gardens around the world. Even if you cannot grow all the plants, I hope you will be inspired to embrace the look and juxtapose verticals, rosettes and spires in your own planting schemes. Most importantly, enjoy!

GLOSSARY OF SOME OF THE TERMS USED IN THIS BOOK

Annual A plant that completes its life cycle in one growing season.

Biennial A plant that, after growing in the first year, flowers and fruits in the second, and then dies.

Continental climate In an area central to a landmass, the seasons are well defined, with hot summers and cold winters.

Divide To propagate plants by division into two or more parts, with root systems intact and one or more shoots.

Dot plant A tall-growing plant used singly in the design of a formal bed to accentuate the contrasts of height, colour and texture.

Glaucous Having a blue-green, blue-grey, grey or white bloom. The term usually refers to stems and leaves.

Lance-shaped or lanceolate Describes a leaf that is broadest below the centre, tapering to a narrow tip, its length three to six times its width.

Maritime climate Although in a maritime climate there is greater exposure to strong sea or ocean winds than in a continental climate, seasonal temperatures are moderate throughout the year, and the rainfall is reliably regular.

Monocarpic Describes plants that flower or fruit only once, before dying. Normally nature makes sure that there are plenty of baby plants clustering around the old plant to continue the line.

Perennial This term normally applies to a non-woody plant that survives for three or more seasons.

Sharp drainage Excess water drains very freely through sharply drained soil.

Strap-shaped Describes a narrow leaf with straight or curving sides, its length six or more times its width.

Subtropical zone A zone between tropical and temperate, having high temperatures with rainfall as heavy downpours in monsoon season.

Succulent A plant that has adapted leaves, roots, or stems for water storage. It is usually native to arid areas.

Temperate zone A zone between tropical and polar, with distinct seasons and rainfall throughout the year.

Exotic inspiration

PREVIOUS PAGES *Aloe vera*.
RIGHT Pointed and paddle-shaped
foliage creates a lush, subtropical
atmosphere in New Jersey, as
opposed to the arid succulent
sharp gardening look. *Alocasia
sanderiana* is in the foreground on
the left, in front of *Asplenium
nidus,* with *Ensete ventricosum*
(syn. *Musa ventricosa*) behind.

Exotic inspiration

The development of the sharp style from the subtropical gardens of the past

Gardeners thrive on challenge. Until the fashion for treating gardens as outside rooms, the British have always looked at their gardens as spaces in which to grow plants, and often taken the view that the more unusual the latest offering is, and the harder it is to grow, the better. No keen horticulturist or gardener worth his salt is able to get enough of the newest plant discovery. Couple a plant's novelty value with suspense as to its hardiness and the effect is compelling. Your horticultural achievements are indisputably greater if you can overcome the challenge of growing tender blooms outside. In the past, even if this were not possible, the rich were wealthy enough to be able to have a hothouse collection going at full tilt in winter, or at least a heated greenhouse or conservatory, so as to enjoy the pleasures and challenges of growing exotic plants indoors.

EXOTIC DISCOVERIES

Although the English excel at gardening, the native flora is limited, and exotic plants have long been highly sought-after. The discovery and widespread dispersal of many spiky exotic plants in Europe and the United States, particularly yuccas and agaves, depended on the Spanish conquest of the Americas in 1521. Seizing on the plants' uniqueness, European horticulturists started to bring back agaves and yuccas almost immediately. *Yucca filamentosa* became a favourite of the royal gardener John Tradescant. Yuccas were reported as flowering in England and the Vatican in the early seventeenth century, and as the east coast of America was colonized more yuccas were discovered and sent back. Agaves were hugely popular in the nineteenth century, when no botanic garden with the right growing conditions was complete without a collection of them. The less hardy agaves were flowering in Salcombe, Devon, towards the end of the eighteenth century. Agaves were especially useful for making fibre, so their commercial potential was realized by planting them in Africa, Indonesia and the Philippines to make rope. Likewise *Agave furcraeoides* was imported to Florida as a fibre crop – a catalyst for further extensive planting of agaves.

Spikes and swords: the giant rosette of *Agave parryi* var. *huachucensis* accompanied by a dasylirion.

The Victorians were intoxicated by the curiosity value of these unique bayonet-like plants from the Americas. In late-nineteenth-century California and Florida, agaves and yuccas captured the popular imagination. The descendants of *Agave attenuata* have freely colonized and today they are almost wild around Los Angeles.

Yuccas and agaves (which will be covered in more detail later) illustrate the fact that to achieve success with exotic plants it helps to understand where the plants you covet originate. Only then can you attempt to replicate the conditions that will ensure the plants' survival – or at least give them a better chance of survival.

There are more than 100 species of agave, over half of which are in Mexico; the rest are found in the US, Central America and the Caribbean basin. Agaves are happy in winter temperatures of $-9\,°C/15\,°F$ if they are in desert dry conditions. An important point about growing agaves and other succulents in temperate climates is that the chief enemy of survival is a combination of cold and wet. Drainage is the key, as their favoured habitats involve drainage among rocks and boulders on hillsides or in gravel on plains in these hot dry areas. Unless the soil is sandy or of porous limestone, most of them cannot tolerate woodland areas and shade. The few species that can be found in a woodland setting rely on thin, stony soil for their survival. If they are located near the coast where rainfall is more generous they colonize cliff faces.

Yuccas are also native to the arid or semi-arid regions of the Americas, with Mexico again as the 'capital', with a wide concentration of varieties. The key to their survival is again sharp drainage. Native to high grasslands in desert regions, species endure extremes of cold and drought. In the western states yuccas thrive on light sandy soils or among rocks and gravel. On the eastern side of the US, where conditions are humid, yuccas flourish on free-draining gravel or sandy soil.

NURTURING THE PASSION

Wealthy nineteenth-century gardeners were able to indulge their love of plants for twelve months of the year. Escaping drab northern European winters by fleeing to the warmth, light, colour and scent of the Mediterranean with flowers in bloom even in winter was a high priority for those who could afford it. Recreating the Med at home by building orangeries and hothouses was the next best substitute. As greenhouse gardening became more sophisticated in Germany and St Petersburg, European interest in exotics soared. Meanwhile, in the more appropriate growing conditions of Italy exotic plants were prized as containerized architectural specimens, their severity ideally suited to the evergreen formal gardens then in vogue.

Then, as now, evergreens were desirable to stave off some of the bleakness of winter. At the most famous and pioneering Mediterranean garden of the nineteenth century, La Mortola, a short hop from Menton over the border into Italy, yucca moths were imported to pollinate Thomas Hanbury's expanding collection of yuccas and consequently the first yuccas in Europe were pollinated there. These and other evergreen spiky plants such as *Dasylirion* and *Nolina* also became the latest must-have plants for conservatories in colder areas and in favoured gardens along the Mediterranean coast.

Gardening one-upmanship escalated out of all proportion at La Mortola. In 1874, Thomas Hanbury, the owner, began a long line of catalogues, *Hortus Mortolensis*, in which he detailed the 103 exotic plants in bloom in the garden in January, and which he sent to *The Gardeners' Chronicle*. In 1886, with 516 plants flowering, he could not resist wondering drily 'whether it was a benevolent act to publish a list of over 500 species of plants blossoming in the open air at a place thirty hours distant by rail, to be read by those compelled to endure the full rigour of a northern winter?' While his catalogues were always a favourite newsworthy feature, in this case the excitement and suspense was heightened because he offered a list of every plant in flower on New Year's Day. But for the edification of other horticultural disciples on the Riviera he also gave a full list of the casualties after a hard winter.

One of Thomas Hanbury's ambitions was to use the garden at La Mortola as a site for acclimatizing subtropical plants. It was firmly believed at the time that once plants were hardened off in the sympathetic climate of the Mediterranean, they would have sufficiently adapted themselves to grow in the temperate conditions of northern Europe. As well as pursuing the Victorian love of growing plants that were both useful and instructive,

Drought-tolerant succulents lend themselves to low-maintenance container gardening.

Thomas Hanbury's aim was to enhance a place of natural beauty by filling it with desirable plants. In 1896 Augustus Hare described it as the most important private garden in Europe, 'more beautiful than anything out of the Arabian Nights'.

Exotic plants also grew bigger and faster than plants 'at home'. Some fast growers excel in the heat. A specimen of *Eucalyptus globulus* was reputed to have grown 17m/60ft, with a girth of 1.5m/5ft, in only seven years at La Mortola. Photograph albums of the period are swollen with pictures of venerable gardeners on the Riviera dwarfed by canopies of succulents.

The rage for exotic plants continued, reaching its apotheosis in the south of France in the late nineteenth and early twentieth centuries. Famous for the mesmeric scenery of the Alpes Maritimes, the sparkling Mediterranean and the unique light, this previously inhospitable region became a winter home for the glamorous rich. Opulent villas gradually peppered the coastline and landscaped gardens often featuring exotic plants were carved out of the rock. Indeed, the rocky promontory on which the Villa Ephrussi de Rothschild on St Jean Cap Ferrat was built had to be blasted with dynamite in order to create the garden. Gardens were often carved out of the hillsides too, as in the case of the Jardin Exotique at Eze, and more famously, the Jardin Exotique in Monte Carlo, created as a tourist attraction, much in the style of a zoological garden for cacti and succulents. As well as the wealthy British who overwintered here, the French themselves were very much in evidence. They followed the fashion for new exotic discoveries. It made sense for wealthy French families who had retired from the tropics to take up residence in the south of France and also create subtropical wonderlands.

Those who could not afford to create such gardens could only dream of them. In *Colour Schemes for the Flower Garden*, written in 1908, Gertrude Jekyll rhapsodizes over one of her ambitions: 'to have a rocky hill-side in full sun, so steep as to be almost precipitous, with walls of bare rock only broken by ledges that can be planted. I would have great groups of Yucca standing up against the sky and others in the rock-face, and some bushes of this great Euphorbia [*characias* subsp. *wulfenii*] and only a few other plants, all of rather large grey effect; Phlomis, Lavender, Rosemary and Cistus . . . it would be a rock garden on an immense scale, planted as Nature plants, with not many different things at a time.' This is pure Riviera gardening.

Although for Jekyll this was a desire never to be fulfilled, she and others could enjoy exotic plants in hothouses. At the Royal Botanic Gardens at Kew in London, the Victorian fascination for the horticultural riches of the tropical world reached its fullest expression in the great Palm House built between 1844 and 1848. Designed to house tropical trees and shrubs, its main purpose was of course to shelter palms. This was followed by the gradual building of the Temperate House in the last forty years of the nineteenth century. Apart from the UK's most favoured locations such as Tresco in the Scilly Isles, the Temperate House is the place to see a mature Chilean wine palm, *Jubaea chilensis*, raised from seed in 1846. The conservatories at Bodnant, Chatsworth and Heligan are famous; many smaller country seats had them too. The enthusiasm for exotic plants has never abated, as the building of the more sophisticated Princess of Wales Conservatory at Kew, divided into ten climatic zones, demonstrates.

Elsewhere in the UK, some gardeners on the western coastline enjoying Gulf Stream influence were quick to see the potential offered by the mild conditions. The west coast might not be the south of France, but there was certainly scope for a bit of make-believe. From Cornwall to the far north-west of Scotland the passion for exotic gardening was developed in various favoured pockets. Frenziedly, gardeners collected hardy palms and tree ferns, rare shrubs and perennials. These gardens began to look distinctly foreign, filled with the most unlikely specimens from all corners of the globe.

When looking back to the early days of these gardens you can learn lessons that are just as relevant today. Wind protection is vital. Although the Abbey Gardens on Tresco are famous for their subtropical plants, the island was exposed to salt-laden gale-force winds crashing in from the Atlantic. The first job for the owner, Augustus Smith, was to build a 3.6m/12ft wall to protect the garden from the west, using the ruined priory walls as protection. There was hardly any vegetation above the height of gorse bushes, so he planted a shelterbelt of trees that would eventually protect the proposed gardens. *Cupressus macrocarpa* and the Corsican pine, *Pinus nigra* subsp. *laricio*, proved to be the toughest in the struggle against salty gales.

Not quite on an island, but almost completely surrounded by the sea, the gardens at Logan, near Stranraer, on the south-western coast of Scotland enjoy an enviable setting, 30m/100ft above sea level. The subtropical climate and Gulf Stream influence make it almost as favourable a location as Tresco. The soil is a slightly acid sandy loam and the plentiful rainfall of 1016mm/40in per annum is evenly spread throughout the year. The problems are similar, however. Exposure to salt winds would scorch foliage without shelterbelts of Sitka spruce (*Picea sitchensis*) and Monterey and Corsican pines (*Pinus radiata* and *P. nigra* subsp. *laricio*). At ground level phormiums illustrate the hardiness of tender spiky plants even in this unlikely corner of the UK. Pittosporum, griselinia and olearia are tolerant of salt winds.

The present development of the garden at Logan began in 1869, when the McDouall family began to demonstrate their love of gardening in this favoured spot. Starting with Agnes McDouall, who passed on her interest to her two sons Kenneth and Douglas, the family transformed the garden into a magical setting for newly discovered species from warm temperate regions. In due course the fruit and vegetable garden came to be the best example of their collecting fervour. In 1909 they planted a long avenue of sixty-two *Cordyline australis*. The avenue

The erupting shark's fin of an agave with *Cordyline australis* 'Albertii' behind, at the Abbey Gardens, Tresco.

was a triumph, until the severe winters of 1962–3 and 1978–9, which left the remaining plants looking distinctly unhappy. So they were removed and in 1980 the avenue was replanted, again from home-grown seed. The original cordylines at Logan had had a good run for their money, having spanned seventy years, which is a couple of active gardening lifetimes: in other gardens how many plantings remain unchanged for seventy years? Because of the fast growth of these plants, even in Scotland, the casual observer does not realize that the present cordylines are replacement specimens. Today they have comfortably reached 6m/20ft.

CONTEMPORARY DEVELOPMENTS

At the beginning of the twenty-first century the enthusiasm for exotic plants has taken on a fervour worthy of the Victorians. Interest in them accelerated in the 1980s when garden designer Myles Challis began experimenting with lush jungly exotics in his south London garden. With the publication of his book *Exotic Gardening in Cool Climates* in 1986, keen gardeners were suddenly made aware that they did not need a mild west-coast garden or indeed a large estate in which to fulfil their dreams. His ground-breaking garden, described in the book, made it clear that many exotics were hardier than presupposed, and that the subtropical look was within reach of more gardeners than had been imagined. Those with sheltered urban gardens were well placed.

In his book *The New Exotic Garden*, published in 2000, Will Giles identifies two styles of exotic planting. In addition to the lush, 'jungle' style, employing plants that enjoy moisture and feeding, such as cannas and hedychiums, there is also the dry, Mediterranean style, which focuses on spiky plants that prefer arid conditions and poor soil, softened by subshrubs such as lavender, rosemary and cistus. Both styles lend themselves to urban microclimates. Nevertheless, in north Norfolk, about a mile from the coast, East Ruston Old Vicarage is a robust example of British plantsmen gardening as if they are on the Amalfi coast rather than in the teeth of Siberian winds.

Veteran gardening luminaries Christopher Lloyd and Beth Chatto have provoked the popular imagination further with their gardens and books. Wanting a change in the old rose garden at Great Dixter, Lloyd's garden in East Sussex, Lloyd and his head gardener Fergus Garrett created a new late-season lush subtropical area instead. Relying on exuberant subtropical foliage, with flower colour provided by cannas and dahlias, the garden transcends the idea of what it meant to have an 'exotic garden' in the UK.

Plantswoman Beth Chatto has been promoting the idea of growing plants without extra watering and

LEFT Spheres and spikes: *Allium cristophii* with a yucca.
RIGHT Swords of *Iris* 'Jane Phillips' with yuccas, grasses and low, fluffy mounds during late May in the gravel garden at Beth Chatto's garden at Elmstead Market, Essex.

annual top-dressing in her dry Essex gravel garden since 1991. She favours drought-tolerant plants which can fend for themselves. Since no extra watering is offered, these plants have to be tough. Many of these resemble round buns in shape, such as lavenders, santolina and ballotas, but Beth also stresses the importance of adding 'dramatic accent plants', and grows many of the spiky flowers and leaf shapes that are hallmarks of sharp gardening. The purple and silver thistle flowers of eryngiums and the majestic cardoon thistle (*Cynara cardunculus*) and *Onopordum acanthium* add spikes and bristles to the naturalistic scheme. She makes the point that yuccas 'make sharp, spiky accents against soft cloudlike shapes of grey'. To ensure a cohesive design she plants in bold, confident groups.

A younger generation of garden designers continues the theme. In London Declan Buckley and Jason Payne specialize in planting exotics in London and the south-east. Paul Spracklin in Essex has also succumbed to both the dry and lush exotic looks. I seem to be unable to create a design without at least one spiky exotic plant. On the west coast of the United States designers such as Richard Hartlage in Seattle, Isabelle C. Greene and Mary Effron in California and Christy Ten Eyck in Arizona embrace the theme.

Public projects also provide exotic inspiration. At the Eden Project, which opened in 2001 with enormous domed conservatories shaped into honeycombed biomes, the planting is specialized for each particular conservatory: so there is a humid tropical biome filled with plants from Africa and South America, while its smaller neighbour houses a vast subtropical collection from the Mediterranean, California and South Africa.

In Sunderland a new rotunda-like conservatory opened in 2001, with a massive waterfall and division of plants into dry or lush exotics. The paths underneath massive tree ferns have dinosaur imprint, reminding the visitor of the age of the plants. Hot on Sunderland's tail, the Sheffield Winter Garden, which opened in December 2002, is one of the largest temperate glasshouses to be built in the last 100 years. It houses an absorbing collection of over 150 species. Sheffield is rightly proud of this final instalment of its Heart of the City project. The planting is reminiscent of the great Victorian planthunting days. Southern hemisphere exotics predominate, with giant palms from Central America, China and Madagascar, grass trees from Australia and Norfolk Island pines.

Whether or not we believe that the warmer and less seasonal climate is thanks to global warming, there is no doubt that plants that were once thought to be tender are now able to withstand UK winters. When Angus White began his Sussex nursery in 1990, specializing in hardy exotics, he opened up the opportunities for gardeners in the UK to experiment with tender exotics in the right places and today exotic plants have never been so widely available. In the USA, as cities such as Las Vegas, Phoenix and Tucson expand, the need to grow drought-tolerant plants has improved the selection of agaves, dasylirions, nolinas and yuccas in cultivation. The export of frost-hardy plants is now big business for Italian nurseries. We have created a demand. With more gardeners prepared to take risks, tropical adventurousness is here to stay. Thomas Hanbury would be lost for words.

Cordylines look infinitely better when planted in groups. The two in the centre here in a London garden are *Cordyline australis* 'Atropurpurea', with *Phormium* 'Yellow Wave' in the foreground. Note how the wire ball sculpture on a pedestal and rounded topiary accentuate the crispness of the sword-shaped leaves.

Swords & lances

PREVIOUS PAGES *Melianthus major.*
RIGHT *Pachpodium lamerie*, with an
agave to the left, in Miami. Let these
silhouettes of soaring spires, hard spiny
barbs, fan shapes and piercing daggers
influence your own style of planting.

Swords & lances

Architectural foliage plants to create the backbone of the design

When designing a garden, how best to start?

A clever design has structure and incorporates accent plants. These focus the eye and create a more interesting garden. It also entails repetition of the chosen theme – as the presence of similar shapes throughout the planting unifies the garden – and should include contrast.

More gardeners are seeing the attractions of sharp foliage plants: plants with leaves in the form of brazen swords and sharp lances, described in this chapter, or with spiky leaves growing in a rosette formation, described in the next chapter. Many of these are evergreens, which provide structure; and, while some evergreens can look dull – indeterminate blobs of leaden green hunkering down at the back of borders, trouble free but predictable and uninspiring – sharp foliage plants look good all year round, lifting the spirits every day. They also make good focal points – lances in particular. Sharp foliage plants have a personality all their own and create contrast with other plants. Moreover they add undeniable drama, and I think this is where their main appeal lies. And of course they add an exotic feel to the garden, conjuring up an atmosphere of sultry days and a subtropical landscape; they can transform your garden into an imaginary holiday destination.

So first choose plants that will provide your focal point and evergreen structure, deciding which of the plants described here appeal to you, and work down from there.

Large specimens create height and draw the eye, so depending on your budget, buy the largest plants you can afford for your focal points. This is one of the great advantages of working with spiky plants. Usually when choosing plants it is better to select young ones as they develop quickly. But with sharp gardening you can buy them big. Larger plants, especially some of the more tender exotic evergreens, have a better chance of survival if you buy them mature, and they immediately introduce a sense of maturity in a brand-new garden or planting scheme. Many nurseries capitalize on this, and large specimens are readily available. As the first six months are the hardest for any plant, it is best to plant them by midsummer to enable them to establish themselves by winter.

THE LARGEST LANCES

These introduce vertical thrust as well as evergreen structure. Palms, although pricey, are an obvious choice as focal points, as they create height. They will tower above lower-storey plants and create an evergreen framework which you can then create contrasts with or echo.

Most people associate palm trees with the glamour of faraway locations and many long to grow a palm tree in their garden; they conjure up the exotic. Even so, some palms are hardy. One of the hardiest palms, *Trachycarpus fortunei*, the Chusan palm, comes from subtropical Asia, and is fully hardy to −15°C/5°F, tolerating frost and snow. Since its introduction by Robert Fortune in 1849, it has proved to be one of the hardiest palms. Specimens in Bulgaria are reported as having survived −28°C/−18°F. It is frequently seen, reaching 9m/30ft or more, in country house gardens planted in the nineteenth century. It was a dream plant for Victorians who favoured the subtropical style of gardening. Still rightly popular with garden designers today, the Chusan palm is widely planted, strangely enough often looking at home with lilacs and laburnums in neighbouring gardens. Fortunately it is tailor-made for an urban garden, as it requires shelter from high winds. It will take at least five years to grow from a 30cm/1ft specimen to 2m/7ft, so if time is short, jump the clock and buy a mature specimen for an instant effect. The enormous (75cm/30in up to 1.2m/4ft across) fan-like dark green leaves are prone to tearing and shredding, so although it is seen in mild seaside gardens, it cannot be grown on a blustery seafront. It throws out yellow panicles of flowers from among the lower leaves, but the foliage is the thing. Its trunk – always solitary, rather than clump-forming – is hairy, with fibres that become matted with age.

Although it looks like a sun-lover, it will tolerate partial shade; and it is best planted in well-drained, rich clay soil, as long as it is never waterlogged. Its leaves may be big but the dense upright habit makes it a useful plant for a confined space, which perhaps explains why it crops up frequently in urban courtyard gardens.

A near relation, and a more practical plant, as it does not have the same large leaves which become ragged in windy gardens, is *Trachycarpus wagnerianus*. Introduced by a German gardener from Japan to Europe in the early twentieth century, it is probably a Chusan palm cultivar, as it has never been recorded in the wild. The more rigid and compact leaves reach 45cm/18in. Although this palm has more practical characteristics, and is in many ways a more manageable palm, it could be more widely planted. Also known as 'waggies', these pocket-sized Chusan palms can be found in specialist nurseries. Under the right conditions – with warmth, good food and drink – they can grow 30cm/12in in the growing season.

If you have a very sheltered garden, look out for *Trachycarpus martianus*, from north-east India and Nepal. It is more prone to wind damage than *T. fortunei*, but it is a more elegant and handsome plant, with glossy mid-green fan-shaped leaves and a smooth trunk which remains smooth. A mature plant can reach 12m/40ft. It has white flowers.

Useful for creating height, pseudopanax are fast becoming the darlings of the plant kingdom for some garden designers. These evergreen trees and shrubs, from New Zealand, Tasmania and

Trachycarpus fortunei, the Chusan palm.

Chile, frost hardy if given good drainage, have viciously toothed leaves and for the sharp garden two of them are must-have plants. The sharply toothed leaves of *Pseudopanax ferox* associate well with other spiny-leaved plants. Resembling a bottle-brush, this evergreen tree's leaves, which can reach 45cm/18in long, emerge horizontally from the main stem, drooping with age. The jaggedly toothed foliage looks somewhat metallic, being a dark bronze-green with an overlay of white or grey. The tree stays columnar, reaching 5m/15ft in time and spreading to 2m/7ft wide. The tip ends in a point when young, but becomes more rounded as it matures. Dark green-leaved *P. crassifolius* is similar, reaching 6m/20ft in height, with a similarly narrow columnar habit, becoming round-headed with age. These trees do not branch till they are mature, so the long leaves emerge straight from the stem, which makes them look weird. Both are frost-hardy and best planted in spring in a sheltered spot. Designer James Fraser uses them to great effect, as revealed on page 185 (and illustrated on the back cover). Both trees introduce an extra-terrestrial feeling into the garden.

Some of the largest lances are the leaves of phormiums, New Zealand flax, erupting at ground level. There are two species: *P. tenax* and *P. cookianum*, and most cultivars have been bred in New Zealand, several famous ones by Margaret Jones. Think of *P. tenax* as an eruption, *P. cookianum* as a fountain.

The grey-green leaves of *P. tenax* soar up to 3m/10ft in the air. Besides being fashionable, they are a source of a fibre which has long been used in the same way as sisal and hemp. Belying their subtropical appearance, most phormiums are frost hardy. Established clumps should tolerate temperatures down to −12°C/10°F, especially if planted in spring with the addition of a 5cm/2in mulch in autumn. They prefer moist, well-drained soil in full sun and their growth rates escalate when watered generously in the growing season. In one wet summer, where it seemed to rain on a daily basis, some new plantings of mine increased tenfold. Bear in mind that it is sensible not to plant them by water, as if the roots freeze they may die. They were once regarded as seaside plants, but a succession of milder winters in Britain means that they are becoming year-round fixtures.

Phormiums make their presence felt in countless ways. By planting these evergreen lances you immediately change the planting rhythm. Because their leaf shape is so arresting, they focus the eye, which absorbs but rushes over rounder plants and sees the phormium's upright leaves as punctuation marks. As *P. tenax* makes fans from ground level, consider growing specimens where

LEFT TO RIGHT *Phormium tenax*, *P. tenax* Purpureum Group and *P.* 'Yellow Wave'.

the fan can be seen to best advantage, perhaps flanking the top of some steps. The drainage will be better at the top of a slope too.

Their flowering spikes add further drama, reaching up to 4.5m/15ft. The burgeoning buds look as tantalizing as budding strelitzias for a few days. Once they are completely open, however, some of the excitement evaporates, for the flowers are merely a dullish red. In their native New Zealand they are pollinated by small birds rather than bees, so brightly coloured flowers are not essential. The seedpods, held upright on *P. tenax*, which hang down like runner beans on *P. cookianum* hybrids, are often the colour of dark chocolate. These wear away gradually during winter, but the stems seem indestructible. When you have tired of them by late winter, remove them.

So phormiums are best grown for their foliage, especially as no other frost-hardy foliage plant offers such a wide variety of coloured leaves. The hardiest, *P. tenax*, is grey-green; it's also the most vigorous and ultimately the largest. But with warm yellow-variegated stripes to hot spicy reds and pinks, darkest purples, creams and golds all available, it seems a pity to limit yourself to the plainest form, unless you have other variegated plants with which they will clash. *P. tenax* 'Variegatum' has creamy yellow stripes at the margins and is easily obtainable, but it's worth looking out for *P. tenax* 'Veitchianum', which is more striking with broad, creamy white stripes. Some words of advice about phormiums:

- Although beguiling and highly coveted, the pink-striped forms are the least hardy. They are also the most slow-growing, so unless you have a sheltered spot, grow them on in containers for a couple of years and protect in winter before planting out. Or, if you are impatient, pay more and invest in a larger specimen, which will have a better chance of survival.
- Many of the pink- and red-striped bronze 'Maori' (syn. 'Rainbow') hybrids have a tendency to revert to a dull bronze in only a few years. You are left with either a more vigorous bronze form or a plant with several leaves that have uneven variegations (with the plain colour dominating). Neither is what you had anticipated. It seems silly to be forced to remove leaves on a plant grown for its foliage, so bear this in mind. However, you may wish to take a chance. *P.* 'Maori Chief', when planted where it can catch the late afternoon sun with the light gleaming through the red and pink stripes, makes a striking image.

ABOVE Flowering phormium with bobbing echinops thistles behind.
BELOW Repetitions of phormiums used as focal points unify this border.

P. tenax Purpureum Group cultivars can also lose their purple-black foliage in favour of more dominant muddy chocolate colours. Select the named cultivar *P.* 'Bronze Baby' which is a dwarf, reaching no more than 1m/39in in height. For a rich dark ebony, *P.* 'Platt's Black' is the one to have.

The upright habit of *P. tenax* and some hybrids makes them useful plants to compartmentalize a large space, as 'room-dividers', or for allées. However, if you have a town garden only 9m/30ft x 6m/20ft, a plant that will ultimately have a 2m/7ft spread needs careful placing, perhaps in a corner or to screen a compost heap. As the fan-shaped leaves splay out it can block the view from windows or trip you up if placed too near a path. If phormiums do get in the way remember that the sword-like leaves will look ridiculous if pruned halfway down. If you have an existing problem and wish to retain the plant, it's a good idea to thin out at least a third of the oldest leaves to ground level. Where space is limited, consider growing several of these sword-like plants together, where the vertical thrust ensures that they take up less ground space.

P. cookianum, the only other species, has lax, arching leaves which extend to 1.2m/4ft. The overall effect is of a much smaller plant, reaching 1m/39in high, more with mature specimens. While it maintains the fan-like habit, the arching leaves cover the base of the plant. This is useful and desirable, as the dying leaves are hidden and can be left unpruned (on *P. tenax*, dead leaves need to be removed as they are not hidden). The lax arching leaves also produce a softer, more elegant effect, which makes them easier to place among other plants. They grow through other plants more easily than those of *P. tenax*, which is more exclamatory.

Hot and cool foliage colours create different moods. A good cool-looking variegated clone, and one of the hardiest, is *P. cookianum* subsp. *hookeri* 'Tricolor', whose leaves are a generous 7.5cm/3in across, striped pale yellow alternating with green, with a thick band of green predominating in the centre. The third colour is a purplish-red margin running down the edge of each leaf. This is a resilient and attractive cultivar, and one to seek out. *P. cookianum* subsp. *hookeri* 'Cream Delight' was found as a sport

Phormiums looking grass-like: **LEFT TO RIGHT** *Phormium tenax lineatum* and *P.* 'Evening Glow'.

of 'Tricolor' by the New Zealand nurserywoman Margaret Jones. The central section of the leaf is predominantly cream, with green stripes near the margins. It illuminates the border without the cream looking anaemic. Lighting up an area which is in shadow for part of the day, it bounces back whatever brightness there is.

P. 'Yellow Wave' has the same lax, arching habit of P. *cookianum* and is equally cheerful, but it is predominantly gold rather than cream, with similar green stripes. It is prone to rust in damp climates. When several leaves become unsightly, which usually happens by midsummer, snip out the offenders with a sharp pair of scissors.

There are some dwarf cultivars, such as P. 'Surfer', but it seems a pity to seek out the tinier forms of a genus that is coveted for its splendid, large, lance-like foliage and ability to conjure up illusions of the subtropics.

The pH level of the soil is not an issue with phormiums, but soil texture may be: the pink-striped forms are less able to cope with heavy clay soil, especially if it is prone to waterlogging. The plain green P. *tenax* may be happy in these conditions.

Although I'm as keen as mustard about phormiums, it grieves me to say that when planting them you need to bear in mind their ultimate size and spread. This is because they have to be thinned rather than pruned back, and are difficult to move if wrongly sited; if they are moved once established, they take time to recover. So it's important to choose the right spot in the first place and to get the spacing right. Place the large, erupting P. *tenax*, with its splayed-out leaves, 2m/7ft apart. The strappier P. *cookianum* will be fine with 1m/39in between each plant.

Also known as the New Zealand cabbage palm, *Cordyline australis* makes an excellent faux palm which associates well with phormiums. It offers the sharp gardener a similar spiky silhouette as a palm tree, but is faster growing and cheaper. Mature specimens can reach 6m/20ft, especially in mild and sheltered gardens. Its chief value lies in the explosion of lance-shaped leaves emerging from a straight trunk. Although described as half hardy to frost tender it sails through most

LEFT North London. Erupting *Phormium tenax* 'Veitchianum' contrasted with horizontal tiers of *Aralia elata* 'Variegata'.
RIGHT, TOP TO BOTTOM *Phormium* 'Duet' with penstemon; P. 'Yellow Wave', with elegant arching leaves; the flowering spike of P. *tenax*.

winters happily – you only need to see how many there are planted as single specimens in UK front gardens to realize that cordylines are survivors. Even if they are weakened by frost – possibly dying back to the ground in severe conditions – they usually spring back from the base. Cautious gardeners wrap them in winter. This is to stop rain or snow settling in the middle of the crown and freezing, which severely damages the plant. However, it is best to wait till the severe weather comes before doing this, because if you wrap too early the leaves can't breathe and tend to go soggy. Plant cordylines in the sunniest position you have – they will cope with a little partial shade and like well-drained soil.

In early summer mature cordylines throw out richly scented plumes of flowers followed by berries. The plain green-leaved cordyline is the most vigorous and hardy, but look out for the gorgeously cream-variegated *C. australis* 'Albertii' and 'Torbay Dazzler' and purple-leaved forms such as 'Atropurpurea', 'Purpurea' and 'Purple Tower'. Cordylines look ever so lonely on their own, especially when planted in front gardens looking like a displaced holiday souvenir. Much better to plant three or more, for they make a lot of impact for little effort.

Appropriate only for sheltered gardens, but worth mentioning as it is such a showstopper, is *Doryanthes palmeri*, the spear lily. A perennial succulent from eastern Australia, the spear lily enjoys the conditions of coastal, open eucalyptus forests. If ever there was a candidate for the sharp garden, this is it. The bright green lance-shaped leaves may reach 2.5m/8ft and the flowering stems are even longer (to 4m/13ft), emerging erect and then arching. These will appear on mature plants, involving a wait of up to fifteen years, as masses of tubular, rich red or red-brown flowers 4cm/1½ in long in late spring. It is frost tender, so unless you enjoy a frost-free climate it is best to grow it as a containerized specimen that can be overwintered under glass. It will put up with poor soil, some drought and partial shade.

Cordyline australis in flower with *Trachycarpus fortunei* and thrusting blue echium spires.

LUSH LANCES OF PERENNIAL PLANTINGS

The sharp gardener can make welcome discoveries among the lusher swords and lances, especially in perennials such as cannas and hedychiums. These require more fertile soil, extra feeding and watering. Their lushness contrasts with the more minimal architectural simplicity of palms and phormiums. With their different textures, they provide paddle-shaped foliage that is hard to beat. And, in the case of cannas, hedychiums, crocosmias and gladiolus, exotic and exuberant flowers.

Much of the excitement of cannas lies in their jungly foliage, especially if it is margined with waving stripes. Here is a selection. The collector will soon become absorbed by cannas' different personalities and variety of foliage and flower colour. Flowering in late summer, they are useful to keep the garden going, their often flaming colours appropriate for summer's climax. Their orchid-like flowers are small in proportion to the mass of paddle-shaped foliage, so it pays to concentrate on the foliage colour or variegation. As the foliage can reach 1.8m/6ft in the growing season, you will enjoy it for much longer than the flowers. As cannas are slender in habit, usually no more than 50cm/20in wide, don't deny yourself the temptation to plant them closely to create impact. Seize the opportunity; cannas are not plants to be niggardly with.

You won't be disappointed with the orange-flowered *Canna* 'Striata', which has an exceptional variegation of light green to yellow-green contained in a leaf margined with dark green. Plant it to catch late afternoon sunlight for a memorable translucent effect. *C. indica* 'Purpurea' and *C.* 'Black Knight' have dark purple or bronze leaves which make a formidable contrast to yellow-green foliage.

If you are choosing a canna for near the variegated foliage of other plants, and do not want bronze or purple as contrasts, you may want one with a plain green leaf. There are many to choose from, such as the golden-yellow-flowered *C.* 'King Midas', or salmon-pink-flowered *C.* 'Erebus'. The non-flowering *C. musifolia*, its name referring to its banana-like leaves, makes a powerful subtropical presence with purple-margined dark green leaves growing to 2.75m/9ft.

In the wild cannas grow in moist open areas in forests in tropical North and South America and Asia. They require fertile soil, shelter and full sun to perform best. There is nothing worse than a stunted-looking canna. As they are greedy, and have but a few months in which to reach 1.8m/6ft, indulge them with a monthly feed of potash-rich liquid fertilizer to encourage flowering. Cannas also soak up the heat, so if you are in a cool location, it's essential to kick start them into new growth under glass. This early boost will pay dividends later, especially if you garden in an area with cool springs. If you do not give them this early shot in the arm, they may still be budding and failing to open as the days become shorter and colder. When the show is over in the autumn, dig them up and store them, keeping them just moist while dormant. Alternatively, if you are in a fairly frost-free climate, leave them in the ground under a deep eiderdown of dry mulch.

When you are planting cannas out in the border you will find that they often look more appropriate near the lush glossy, evergreen lances of phormiums and *Trachycarpus fortunei* than the arid-looking spiky swords of agaves and yuccas. Their growing conditions match also.

RIGHT Orange *Canna* 'Tropicanna' ('Phasion') in a Long Island garden. **FOLLOWING PAGES, LEFT TO RIGHT** The sun can create translucent effects on the glorious foliage of the variegated *Canna* 'Tropicanna' ('Phasion'); pointed paddle-shaped foliage and fiery exotic flowers on cannas in Lady Walton's garden, La Mortella, in Ischia.

Hedychiums are also rhizomatous perennials. Known as ginger lilies, they come from the moist, lightly wooded areas of Asia, and have lance-shaped foliage. They look like smaller and more subtle cannas, reaching heights from 1m/3ft to 5m/15ft, with the same upright habit. They echo the exuberant foliage of cannas, without having the choice of variegations or different-coloured leaves. Most of them have mid-green leaves with more subdued tones of orange-red, yellow or white flowers, also flowering in late summer. You could echo cannas with hedychiums and use them to create a more restful atmosphere in a shadier area, as they tolerate partial shade. They appreciate the same good living as cannas, so treat them to a monthly dose of liquid fertilizer at the same time. As they are slightly hardier (frost hardy to frost tender), you can consider leaving some of the frost-hardy ones out in winter, as long as they are bedded down beneath a thick mulch. But as with cannas they appreciate heat early the following season to trigger them into action, and if you are unsure it is best to dig them up in winter and kick start them the following spring and early summer under glass, especially in cooler northern areas of the UK, where the summer takes a while to get into its stride. Without this boost they somehow never manage to catch up, even by late summer. As with cannas, if you do decide to lift hedychiums, keep them just moist in the winter.

I would plant both cannas and hedychiums in a spot where you will find it easy to water them with a liquid fertilizer because you will be less inclined if they are too far down the garden. Cannas look great from my kitchen window, and receive copious draughts of old washing-up water. Hedychiums are best sited near a path or terrace for their exotic fragrance.

Two of the frost-hardy ones (to −5°C/23°F) are *Hedychium coccineum* 'Tara', which is orange with red stamens, growing to 3m/10ft and spreading to 1m/39in, and *H. forrestii*, useful if you would like to introduce some white flowers and growing to 1.5m/5ft with a spread of 60cm/2ft. The more tender half-hardy *H. gardenerianum* can reach 2m/7ft, spreading to 1m/39in, with fragrant lemon-yellow flowers and bright red stamens, and is best overwintered under glass.

The foliage of cannas and hedychiums looks at home near the paddle-shaped leaves of the Abyssinian banana, *Ensete ventricosum*, a banana-like perennial which can reach up to 6m/20ft high in a warm climate once mature. It is one of the most striking of exotic specimens. The sturdy foliage is far less prone to being shredded by the wind as the musa bananas are. Its immense leaves also associate well with the finely cut foliage of palms such as *Trachycarpus fortunei*, or the European dwarf fan palm, *Chamaerops humilis*, over which it will tower.

It looks at its best surrounded by the lusher-looking exotics, rather than drought-lovers, and, as its appearance suggests, it prefers the good life of humus-rich soil and a monthly dose of liquid fertilizer. You can reserve your sunniest spot for other plants, as *Ensete ventricosum* prefers midday protection from the sun. When you lift it for the winter, cut back the long roots and brace yourself to cut back the foliage to the newest handful of leaves. Don't cut the dead leaves lower than the base of each leaf blade. The enormous specimen in the exotic south London garden of garden

RIGHT, TOP TO BOTTOM Scented *Hedychium gardnerianum* in flower; *Ensete ventricosum* 'Maurelii'; *E. ventricosum* (syn. *Musa ensete*). FAR RIGHT In this New Jersey garden a containerized *Ensete ventricosum* 'Maurelii' is treated as an annual and pitched out at the end of the season.

designer Myles Challis has been planted with roofing felt around the rootball, to stave off some of the winter wet. He had to leave it in the ground as it became too large to dig up and overwinter. The plant is now encased in a glass pyramid frame, heated with a fan heater on a timer.

The dark red-leaved form *E. ventricosum* 'Maurelii' is the one to track down, as the deep colour adds a velvety richness few other plants can match. Grown for its huge paddle-shaped leaves this frost-tender perennial is hardy to 7°C/45°F. Spectacular in a subtropical scheme and resembling a banana palm, this is lushness on a grand scale. It is found growing on the mountain slopes of Asia and tropical Africa. Treat it as a foliage plant because the banana-like fruits are dry and unpalatable. It is fast-growing and requires humus-rich soil in full sun or partial shade. Regular monthly liquid feeds develop the foliage so that by late summer and autumn, it will have reached a maximum of 6m/20ft. In frost-prone areas it is essential to lift the plant for winter, pruning the leaves and roots and storing it in a frost-free environment, keeping it just moist.

One of the sharpest-looking leaves is not sharp at all. It is useful in sharp gardening as a contrast to vertical sword-shape foliage. In spite of its highly serrated leaf margins (reminiscent of a circular saw blade), South African *Melianthus major* is lettuce-leaf soft. The glory of *M. major* is its unique, fresh unfurling foliage, glaucous and pinnate. Reaching a height of 1.5m/5ft by autumn, it casts dramatic, highly toothed shadows. It makes a beautiful and eyecatching foliage plant, with the unexpected odour of peanut butter when rubbed. It is best enjoyed from mid- to late summer, when the foliage is at its height, so it ties in well with the bold foliage of purple cannas or the *Ensete* mentioned above. Or imagine the grey leaves sandwiched between purple phormiums – sharks' teeth looking as if they are about to rip open the spear-like foliage.

I know of no other perennial that grows as vigorously, and looks so happy, even in early winter. It is best grown in full sun and will benefit from a winter mulch. Although classed as frost hardy, it springs back from the base in spring as long as temperatures have not fallen too far below −5°C/23°F; if the winter is mild and the foliage survives, treat it as an herbaceous perennial and cut it back to the

ground in spring to rejuvenate the foliage. Don't be tempted to chop it down in late winter, as new growth may yet be damaged by late spring frosts. If the plant is not cut back, small unusual brownish flowers will appear the following season, but although they may well be a talking point, they do not enhance the plant's overall appearance. If left unchecked, *Melianthus major* will grow to 3m/10ft, so you could treat it as a tree and clean off the lower leaves. Even so, mature plants can look scruffy at the base, with curled-up dry leaves, so it is best to cut it down annually in spring so that you can enjoy the juvenile foliage at ground level.

LEFT *Melianthus major.* **FOLLOWING PAGES, LEFT TO RIGHT** *Strelitzia reginae,* the bird of paradise flower; *Crocosmia* 'Ember Glow'; *Gladiolus communis* subsp. *byzantinus* with *Allium nigrum* in the background.

Also from South Africa, crocosmias are cormous herbaceous perennials with ridged green lance-shaped leaves. Frost-hardy *C*. 'Lucifer' throws out spikes of brilliant scarlet flowers in midsummer up to 1.2m/4ft tall. Showy and exotic, these last about a month. Crocosmias look at home with flaming cannas, but do not need the same rich diet. By midsummer they have formed a thicket of jostling swords which make their mark until the autumn. It is best to thin out the corms on a regular basis as crocosmias multiply fast and eventually become blind when congested.

You could continue introducing some colour on lance-like foliage with *Gladiolus*, another cormous perennial. Most gladioli originate in South Africa, and enjoy the same conditions as crocosmias – full sun and well-drained soil. Apart from the gladiolus cultivated for floristry, which can look out of place in a border rather than a cutting garden, there are one or two whose sword-shaped leaves add to the sharp look. For scent, plant half-hardy *G. callianthus*, from Mozambique, which has pure white flowers that bloom in late summer and early autumn on 1m/39in spikes. The fully hardy and prolific *G. communis* subsp. *byzantinus*, from north-west Africa, Spain and Sicily, grows to the same height but is deep magenta, flowering from late spring to early summer.

For a quieter effect the frost-hardy rhizomatous perennial *Diplarrhena moraea*, from Australia and Tasmania, is useful in late spring and early summer. It offers restraint in the early-season border before the late-summer glories of fiery cannas and crocosmias. Its evergreen sword-like foliage is dark green to slightly glaucous and echoes the spiky theme of larger neighbours. Its white flowers grow to 60cm/2ft tall. Make sure that it does not get overshadowed by leafier plants, as it enjoys well-drained soil in full sun, preferring partial shade in a hot site.

The bird of paradise plant, *Strelitzia reginae*, is a clump-forming evergreen perennial hailing from South Africa. It has become a key plant in the Mediterranean where it survives happily. In frost-prone areas, successfully overwintering strelitzias outside is a forlorn hope, as they need to be kept above 10°C/50°F. Don't despair, however, as they are good in pots and will flower better if they are well rooted and even slightly neglected. *Strelitzia reginae*'s main effect comes from its emerging spiky orange and blue flowers, resembling a crane's head in profile. The luxuriant paddle-shaped green leaves thrust out on elegantly arching stems, usually to 1m/39in tall with the giraffe-like flower rising way above that, to 2m/7ft, making it an unforgettable sight. It needs plenty of moisture and a monthly liquid phosphate-rich fertilizer to reach its potential.

If you hanker after the larger-leaved giants and have a sheltered garden, able to sustain frost-tender plants – where temperatures do not fall below 5°C/41°F, you could bask under the lance-shaped leaves of *Strelitzia nicolai*, which reach up to 10m/30ft in its native South Africa or a similarly warm climate. With 1.5m/5ft long rectangular leaf blades rising on leaf stalks 2m/7ft long, *S. nicolai* is a garden giant suitable for partnering with the extrovert foliage of bananas and cannas. The white flowers are not as show-stopping as those of *S. reginae*, but the foliage more than makes up for this. The large leaves tear with age, but not as much as those on bananas. The ultimate height of *S. nicolai* means that it will require a large container to prevent it from becoming too top heavy and falling over, so if wheeling it in and out in winter and summer you need to consider its portability.

LUSH AQUATIC

If you are designing a sharp garden and wish to create a planting scheme for a pond, it needs to have the appropriate planting to tie in with the plants around it.

The Japanese rush, *Acorus gramineus*, most often found in eastern Asia, makes a fan of semi-evergreen glossy green linear leaves, up to 35cm/14in. I would seek out the variegated form, which is frost hardy (−5°C/23°F), slightly smaller, and bearing stripy cream and yellow leaves.

Acorus calamus 'Variegatus' is bone hardy, with bright green strap leaves striped cream and white, up to 90cm/36in. It is at its best when planted in full sun at the margin of a pond, with water no deeper than 22cm/9in. Grow this plant for its vibrant foliage, which is deciduous, as the flowers are insignificant. It can also be grown in a bog garden, in marshy areas or even in a sink.

Extremely vigorous, and therefore a potential nightmare, the yellow flag iris, *I. pseudacorus*, is widely found in Europe, Asia and north Africa. It has sword-like foliage emerging from a fan, each leaf reaching 90cm/36in. As a marginal or damp soil plant it will colonize an area quickly, so it is only suitable for large ponds or lakes. It needs humus-rich soil, deep, wet and preferably acid.

Nothing reflects as well in water as brightly coloured sword-like leaves or stems, so it is worth seeking out the variegated form *I.p.* 'Variegata', which has yellowish white-striped foliage that reflects well. If a rampant spreader is to be allowed full rein in a large expanse, it is surely better to capitalize on this more interesting variegated form.

With lance-shaped leaves the arum lily from southern and eastern Africa, *Zantedeschia aethiopica*, is an essential marginal aquatic perennial for moist soil. Its tuberous rhizomes luxuriate in the good life – sun and moist, humus-rich soil. Zantedeschias are frost hardy, but protect them against frost with plenty of humus to encourage lush growth the following year. The glossy bright-green leaves are eyecatching enough in themselves, but the flowers that emerge as pure white spathes, from late spring to midsummer, are beguiling.

LEFT, CLOCKWISE FROM TOP Swords of *Iris pseudacorus* 'Variegata'; an iris rill with the darker *I. sibirica* 'Tropic Night' and the lighter *I. laevigata* in wire-mesh baskets; *Pontederia cordata*. **RIGHT, TOP TO BOTTOM** *Iris pseudacorus* 'Variegata'; *Zantedeschia aethiopica*.

SPIKES FOR SHADE

Few gardeners can boast that they have no shade in their gardens. So what do you do if you have filled all your sunny areas with spikes and lances and have a gaping shady area to fill? It looks odd if you have a different style of planting, so here are some ideas for plants that can be grown in shade and sustain the theme.

Shade comes in different forms, from that created by high buildings and walls to that beneath overhanging branches. When there are walls it often means that the ground below is dry. The ground underneath overhanging branches will be even drier, because of the leaf canopy and root competition. Tough conditions such as this require tough plants. Dry shade can also mean dusty, so planting some glossy foliage, which stays shiny, will pay dividends in awkward places.

The evergreen terrestrial British native fern *Asplenium scolopendrium*, the hart's tongue fern, with upstanding pointed leaves, offers perhaps one of the glossiest greens of all for deep or partial shade. Use it as a ground-cover plant, as its strap-shaped leaves reach up to 40cm/16in. These evergreen leaves begin to look tatty, blotched with black, by late winter, but they soon start rejuvenating from shuttlecock crowns in spring: the fronds starting to unfurl in early spring is one of the most beautiful of spring pictures. At first they look good enough to eat but they settle into leathery middle age by

ABOVE *Asplenium scolopendrium* Crispum Group.

midsummer. You can cut off offending old leaves but if you don't have time they seem to self-destruct within a month. The great thing about these ferns is their ability to endure any amount of neglect yet still look abundantly healthy; they will tolerate just about anything, barring full sun all day. They can self-seed into any available crack in a wall and survive on practically nothing.

Aspleniums look good planted underneath mahonias, their glossy foliage contrasting with the matt, darker green of the mahonias. One of the best of these shrubs is *M. lomariifolia*, from western China, which within a decade can make a shrub 3m/10ft high and almost as wide. Mahonias have pinnate dark green leaves, with lance-shaped sharply toothed leaflets. When you need winter colour, mahonias are perfect, flowering from late autumn well into winter. If the fragrant 20cm/8in brilliant yellow flowers are left unpruned, the blue-black berries which follow, hanging in clusters like fairy grapes, are just as welcome. Also from China, *M. japonica* 'Bealei' is shorter and bulkier, reaching 2m/7ft high and 3m/10ft wide with more blue-green leaves and tighter, erect pale yellow racemes. *M. x media* is a lemon-yellow flowering cross between *M. lomariifolia* and *M. japonica*, reaching 5m/16½ft and 4m/13ft wide.

ABOVE, LEFT TO RIGHT *Mahonia* x *media* 'Charity' in flower with a pyracantha; *M. aquifolium* (left) and *Helleborus foetidus*.

Spikes and lances to create grand-scale structure

Abbotsbury subtropical garden in Dorset has a long-standing maturity from which impatient gardeners can draw inspiration. It seems likely that the first of its Mediterranean plantings was introduced in 1899 after the head gardener had spent ten years in La Mortola on the Riviera. With 8 hectares/20 acres, much of it woodland, the site offers plenty of shelter. The mild seaside climate, protection from surrounding woodland and plentiful south-coast sunshine create conditions which any self-respecting lover of spiky foliage will be happy to drool over. The garden has always played on the subtropical theme, but now there are several areas which have recently been transformed with great vigour, using plantings of spiky swords and lush lances.

Head gardener Stephen Griffiths has rounded up many of the usual suspects. From July onwards the pageant of hot summer colour is beginning to crystallize and by late summer and autumn the profusion of foliage is at its height. Although this is gardening on a grand scale, there are dozens of valid and usable examples which can inspire the smaller plot. A smaller plot does not necessarily mean that everything has to be down-scaled: often the effect is more telling if over-scaled plants are used. I don't believe in 'small garden, small plants'.

At Abbotsbury, palms are used to create a backbone of planting, around which everything else can be developed. Although the Dorset coastline is more damp Mediterranean than subtropical, an exotic effect has been achieved by growing plants able to cope with the occasional sub-zero temperatures.

Trachycarpus fortunei is the elderly lynchpin in much of the garden, with 100-year-old specimens now topping 20m/66ft. Stephen has added more tender palms such as *Butia capitata*, *Phoenix canariensis* and the European dwarf fan palm, *Chamaerops humilis*. The faster-growing cabbage palms, *Cordyline australis*, are also used to add height. All these palms punctuate the planting with their size, adding bulk and weight.

Great fun can be had from echoing these larger architectural specimens. The yellow-variegated *Cordyline australis* 'Torbay Dazzler' has an underplanting of *Phormium* 'Yellow Wave', which picks up the spikiness and colours of the cordyline's foliage. The half-hardy castor oil plant, *Ricinus communis*, grown here as summer bedding, is used often to punctuate swords and lances. Its glossy palmate bronze-red foliage makes a bold contrast especially with narrow spikes, and as the leaves can reach 45cm/18in across, they are also in proportion with the larger-than-life subtropical effect. They are perfect planted among cordylines and *Trachycarpus fortunei*.

Planted up against the veranda of the colonial-style tea rooms is a border including the frost-tender palm *Butia capitata*, juxtaposed with the evergreen swords of a *Phormium* 'Apricot Queen', glaucous serrated *Melianthus major* and hedychiums. *Ricinus communis* and the variegated *Fatsia japonica* with similar

Spikes and fluffy plants are contrasted in this grouping at Abbotsbury, which includes a flowering *Beschorneria yuccoides*, *Phoenix canariensis* in the top right-hand corner and the green-and-yellow-striped *Yucca gloriosa* 'Variegata'. The raised bed, made with upended sleepers, provides the required drainage for the beschorneria.

foliage echo each other and contrast with the other plants. The feathery transparent fronds of *Butia capitata* are especially useful as you can look through them to other plants, while it is still 2m/7ft high. By planting it near a building Stephen has effected an insurance against severe cold snaps, as the building offers more protection than open ground.

A simple but good grouping involves the jagged outline of *Trachycarpus fortunei*, underplanted with a vertically thrusting *Phormium* 'Apricot Queen' and broad paddle-shaped *Ensete ventricosum*. The three different forms complement each other perfectly.

The rounded habit of the Japanese mock orange, *Pittosporum tobira*, makes a shrubby foil at ground level for cordylines. The cordylines' straight trunks and spiky mop heads are given ballast by the bun-shaped pittosporums. The pittosporum here has large, obovate, glossy, deep green leaves which also contrast with the cordylines' matt foliage. The rounded habit of

the leaf formation and the shrub itself provides a cushion over which the cordylines tower. *Pittosporum tobira* also flowers prolifically with masses of bell-shaped, highly scented, creamy white flowers in early summer.

By late summer the planting of the banana palm, *Musa basjoo*, with *Melianthus major* has come into its own. The lax, heavily serrated pinnate leaves of the melianthus, reaching 1m/39in, echo the arching musa foliage 2m/7ft above. The musa leaves, shredded by wind, almost as soon as they unfurl, are equally ragged. Repetition of shape and habit, and contrast in colour between the glaucous and the green leaves, make this an effective combination.

More plantings at Abbotsbury. **LEFT** Repetition of colour and foliage using different plants: swords of *Cordyline australis* underplanted with phormiums. **RIGHT** Spires of *Kniphofia* 'Bees Sunset' in the foreground with flowering spikes of *Acanthus spinosus* to the left and *Melianthus major* to the right. Wedding-cake tiers of *Cornus controversa* 'Variegata' in the background introduce horizontal lines.

Exotic urban oasis

Philip Gibson's garden in north London shows how a subtropical effect can be achieved in an urban garden. The long narrow plot is 35m/115ft x 15m/49ft. Relying to some extent on London's microclimate, designer Jason Payne worked out a formula that would meet Philip's brief for an exotic oasis filled with spiky drama. Lacking the woodland protection of Abbotsbury's twenty acres, the garden needed a shelterbelt. So Jason introduced a grove of fast-growing *Eucalyptus nitens*, *E. perriniana* and *Pinus radiata* at the furthest end of the garden, which opens to a park. They provide shelter on two levels, at 10m/33ft and 3m/10ft respectively. The trunks have been cleaned off to prevent the borders below from becoming too shady. As in the wild, these trees filter the wind, and in a garden setting they create privacy by being evergreen.

In a flat garden it is imperative to enhance the drainage for half-hardy and frost-hardy plants, so Jason created slightly raised beds throughout, adding plenty of grit for drainage before and during planting. This was especially important here, as the combination of clay soil and a high water table can lead to occasional flooding. Up-ended pieces of Derbyshire sandstone roughly 30cm/12in higher than the lawn and paths contain each bed. Weed-suppressing breathable plastic sheeting was placed on the pathways; and pea shingle thrown down on it. A stepping-stone arrangement of cut flags, placed randomly, make simple paths. To emphasize the sense of perspective, the flags become smaller at the far end of the garden.

Frost sweeps down from nearby Primrose Hill and the garden is a frost pocket. As Philip sees no point in looking at plants that have to be shrouded with fleece for most of the winter, like wrapped Christmas presents, he chose frost-hardy evergreens, which would have a good chance of survival.

Jason's formula was to introduce tried-and-tested reliably hardy palms such as *Trachycarpus fortunei*, *Chamaerops humilis* and *Butia capitata* as the skeleton framework. Yuccas echo this theme at ground level. He then bulked up these true exotics with plants that look subtropical and are also frost hardy, such as large-leaved *Gunnera manicata* and *Darmera peltata*. The gunnera, from Chile, resembles a giant rhubarb. Growing to 2m/7ft or more, with palmate leaves roughly as wide, it contrasts well with the spikes and lances. If a plant originates from Chile, the odds are that it will be frost hardy (to −5°C/23°F). Its size demonstrates that over-scaling is useful in a medium-sized garden. It also helps to blur the edges, so that you cannot see where the garden's boundaries finish, giving

Jagged silhouettes of *Cordyline australis* in Philip Gibson's garden in north London. The informal stepping-stone path in pea gravel works well with this style of planting. Cordylines will take some shade, but the *Eucalyptus nitens* and *E. perriniana*, which provide shelter, have been cleaned of lower branches to allow as much light as possible to filter through.

the illusion that the garden is bigger than it is.

The overall look here is of lush lances and spiky swords thrusting through softer plantings which create a harmonious balance and introduce flowers into the garden. Near the house a large feathery shrub, the Mount Etna broom (*Genista aetnensis*), throws up a fountain of stalks, creating an impression of long blades of grass suspended in the air. It is delicate and transparent, and in summer is transformed by thousands of tiny yellow flowers. You can look through and beyond these leafless stalks to the next instalment of the garden. The less hardy silk tree, *Albizia julibrissin* 'Rosea', creates a similar fuzzy outline, with finely cut pinnate leaves and pink bobble flowers in summer. The drawback of this plant is that English summers are rarely warm enough to ripen the wood sufficiently to allow it to survive a typically cold, moist winter.

Instead of the Satsuki azaleas favoured at Lamorran (see next page), one of the most successful associations with swords and lances is the underplanting of the shrub *Ceratostigma willmottianum*, as it flowers continuously from midsummer to the first frosts. Its deep blue plumbago-like flowers cool the garden down. Resembling a blue froth to about 30cm/12in high, circling the sharp silhouettes, this is a no-nonsense shrub that is pretty hard to beat as low-maintenance filler. If the bare stems die back to the ground in winter it can be rejuvenated in the same way as fuchsias by pruning to the ground in spring. It responds quickly, and will be flowering on the new wood by summer.

Throughout the planting Jason has built up contrasts with interlocking partnerships. So, cordylines and phormiums are offset by spring-flowering scented osmanthus, a rounded, dark green-leaved shrub. Yuccas and the ferociously barbed shrub *Colletia hystrix* (syn. *C. armata*) are softened by the fuzzy outline of corokia, a New Zealand shrub. Or assorted spikes and prickles are thrown together to create an exhilarating combination such as the dwarf fan palm, *Chamaerops humilis*, the spiky slender spire of a juniper and *Grevillea rosmarinifolia*. Grevilleas are prickly to the touch, like junipers, but the overall effect is of a soft-textured shrub. Spiny-leaved mahonia is planted next to *Pinus radiata*, of which every leaf tip is a needle. As well as complementing each other, the spines and needles contrast, as all you see from a distance is the effect of the jagged, barbed mahonia against the fuzzy outline of the pine.

ABOVE Sugar-frosted pleated foliage of *Chamaerops humilis*, the European dwarf fan palm.

Spiky oases in mild coastal conditions

In the southern Cornish garden of Mr and Mrs Dudley-Cooke, at Lamorran House, St Mawes, the garden has been designed to echo the grand and great gardens of the Mediterranean. The conditions are nigh-on perfect. The growing season is virtually all year round and frost is almost unknown, barring a couple of winters. Like most British gardens attempting to create a spiky oasis reminiscent of the stretch of coastline from Nice to Menton, the main problem is not cold but winter wet, always more prevalent on the coast; St Mawes enjoys an annual rainfall of just over 1.1m/43in. But the well-drained, sloping south-facing site, mild climate and shelterbelts mean that the Dudley-Cookes have been able to give full rein to their exotic aspirations.

The most memorable planting is a profusion of Chusan palms, *Trachycarpus fortunei*, underplanted with the European dwarf fan palm, *Chamaerops humilis*. The Dudley-Cookes have capitalized on the high rainfall by using Satsuki azaleas almost as a foaming ground cover, contrasting with the fan-like palm leaves above.

My first garden on Cumbria's sheltered south coast demonstrates the effectiveness of growing jagged spiky plants against a horizon of tidal estuary. Cumbria, England's most north-western county, is noted for high rainfall. A few hundred metres from Morecambe Bay, the conditions are moist and mild.

Located on a steep slope, the garden incorporates different self-contained levels. Here was a site that did not need dividing into compartments: the lie of the land sorted that. A walled garden on a higher level than the main garden creates further division and means that some parts of the garden open on to the wide empty expanse of Morecambe Bay, while some areas are more intimate and enclosed, offering glimpses more than a panorama.

In the UK, such a location offers the potential for growing New Zealand and Mediterranean plants. They flourished so well that I began a National Council for the Conservation of Plants and Gardens collection of phormiums here, until I ran out of space. *P. tenax* in particular, in the right conditions, reaches colossal proportions (3m/10ft x 3m/10ft) within a few years.

Cornwall becomes Cannes with the help of these Chusan palms (*Trachycarpus fortunei*) framing the view of St Anthony from Lamorran House, Cornwall.

Often the best garden pictures happen by chance. With the backdrop of tidal estuary beyond – sparkling and shimmering at high tide – a vast expanse of mud and sand at low tide, I noticed that the phormiums' jagged outlines framed the view. They created a subtropical aura and seduced me into imagining I was gardening under warmer skies. I preferred the lushness of phormiums to the more arid, matt textures of yuccas, whose spiky shapes would have been as telling, although the overall effect would not have been as glossy.

Phormiums have long been associated with coastal planting. There are hundreds of ragged examples on promenades from Morecambe to Torquay where a bit of pruning and thinning would work wonders. Ragged or not, their sword-like foliage echoes that of spiky cabbage palms, *Cordyline australis*, which make thick trunks and reach 9m/30ft in the right conditions. Although the large leaves of *Trachycarpus fortunei* are prone to tearing in the wind, precluding it from being a front-line seaside plant, in a sheltered corner of a seaside garden it makes a distinguished

specimen. I found that the lax arching leaves of the *P. cookianum* hybrids associate best with its jagged outline. The thrusting leaves of *P. tenax* merely add more of the same. So I planted *P. tenax* as focal plants, and used *P. cookianum* hybrids for underplanting beneath larger spiky plants such as *Trachycarpus fortunei* and cordylines.

After a few years of growing phormiums, I began to find I preferred the variegated cultivars more than the grey-green species, simply because if you are going to have a large evergreen plant taking up room, it might as well have an interesting colour. And as few evergreen perennials match the colours presented by phormiums, I could not resist taking advantage of some of the pinks, crimsons, ebony blacks, golds and creams available.

The phormium is an all-purpose plant: a well-placed *P. tenax* cultivar, whether it be by a building, in the border, or planted on the edge of a lawn or near a pond, is a striking addition to the garden. However, too many *P. tenax* can create a jarring restless look, so I softened their outline with plants with equally strong shapes. Shiny-leaved *Fatsia japonica* with flat, five-fingered leathery leaves, looking like a giant's gloves, makes a good partner: as the leaves are balanced horizontally on the plant, they contrast with the phormiums' vertical sword-shaped foliage. Alternatively, a shrub that has a fuzzy outline such as *Corokia* x *virgata* from New Zealand, with twisting stems and tiny silvery metallic leaves, makes a more subtle foil.

At my first garden repeated *Phormium* 'Yellow Wave' emerge as tufts among carpets of daisy-flowered osteospermums and fuzzy-shaped Mediterranean rosemary, lavender, artemisias and sages.

SHELTERBELTS

Pines have the double advantage of continuing the spiky theme with their prickly pine needles and providing shelterbelts and windbreaks for frost-hardy and half-hardy plants. Ultimately they will create shade, which will provide different planting opportunities. They enjoy the same conditions as most of the plants already described: well-drained soil in full sun. One of the choicest is the fully hardy Monterey pine, *Pinus radiata*, which will eventually make a narrow conical 25m/80ft tree. Its 15cm/6in long needles are a glossy bright green. *P. montezuma*, a frost-hardy, broadly conical tree, becoming 30m/100ft high and 9m/30ft wide in maturity, is even finer, with longer fresh green leaves up to 30cm/12in long. It is one of the most tactile pines. Many UK coastal resorts have plantings of *P. sylvestris*, the columnar Scots pine, which provide excellent shelter and are impervious to salt-laden gales and high winds, eventually making efficient windbreaks. Their ultimate height is 30m/100ft, with a spread of 9m/28ft. The 7cm/3in leaves have a blue-green tinge.

FUZZY AND CUSHION CONTRASTS

The plants described in this chapter create structure, keeping the eye interested with different shapes and textures: I would describe these as linchpin skeleton plants in a design. But their minimalistic appearance is rather severe on its own. To balance the design other contrasts are required. Ground-hugging rounded subshrubs such as artemisias and santolinas make good decorative foils. Their fluffy cushion shapes seem to bring the sharper plants down to earth and complement them, their solid mass adding ballast at the foot of thrusting verticals above them; swords and lances have all the more impact when planted among them. Fast-growing and short-lived, subshrubs are also useful as temporary quick-fix plants in between maturing evergreens during the early years.

BELOW, LEFT TO RIGHT   The Monterey pine, *Pinus radiata*; *P. radiata* Aurea Group.

Amongst these, Mediterranean-type plants with aromatic foliage are always desirable. Start with the silver filigree foliage of *Artemisia* 'Powis Castle', and then add one or more of the santolinas. Grow the dark green cotton lavender *Santolina rosmarinifolia* as the green varieties have a less coarse appearance than the more well-known silver *S. chamaecyparissus* cotton lavender. The yellow bobble-like flowerheads which appear in midsummer look much better against green than silver leaves. Equally low-mounded, the squat golden barrel cactus, frost-tender *Echinocactus grusonii*, native to central Mexico, forms cushions of golden barrels which contrast well with spiky leaves. I do not reckon much to its survival if planted outside in the UK, however. But you can cheat a little and create the same effect by growing less tender bun-shaped plants. From a distance it is hard to tell the difference between *Echinocactus fruonni* and santolinas, or so I like to kid myself anyway.

Purple or variegated sages also make low rounded domes of foliage, and their matt felty leaves contrast in texture with glossy foliage. A dark-flowering compact lavender such as *Lavandula angustifolia* 'Hidcote' is another useful fluffy supporting player in this context. Osteospermums, with their cheerful daisy flowers in bloom from May to September, although from South Africa, hammer home the Mediterranean theme. All these ground-huggers calm down spiky plantings. The proportions are right for growing with yuccas and the *P. cookianum* cultivars.

For the larger cultivars of *P. tenax*, the same issues apply. Fuzzy shapes act as a relief. Just grow bigger plants, such as shrubby lime-green *Euphorbia characias* subsp. *wulfenii*, which flowers for three months in spring and early summer. The rounded shapes of cistus, rosemary, hebes and *Teucrium fruticans* smooth down a design, provide desirable flowers and allow the vertical accent plants to act as focal points. Many of these fast-growing plants need replacing after five years or so, by which time the phormiums should be taking pride of place: as in all gardens, the appearance continuously evolves. If you have a south- or west-facing wall, grow abutilons against it as a contrast to phormiums: these are also fast-growing (to 3m/10ft) and long-flowering in early summer. Grow purplish-blue-flowered *A. vitifolium* next to plants with gold and cream foliage as the flowers are set off by their neighbours.

These fast-growing Mediterranean plants are much better bought as smaller, and therefore cheaper, plants. The more juvenile the plant, the more vigorous will be its early growth. Sun-loving rosemary, lavender, santolina, euphorbia and cistus often increase their size tenfold in one season if planted in spring, with the growing season ahead of them. Plant in full sun and poor soil. There is no need to add fertilizer; indeed, generous feeding only encourages lush growth and weakens the plant. These subshrubs are best grown hard to withstand a cold soggy winter. They need to develop their own root system in situ, as an insurance policy against drought, and will have a better chance of survival if the growing conditions are hard, as in the wild.

LEFT Bristly cushions of *Echinocactus grusonii* contrast with *Aloe vera* blooms and spears in a formal garden in Arizona. In cooler climates this telling simplicity can be repeated by contrasting bun-shaped lavenders to offset sword-like leaves. **FOLLOWING PAGES** A pin-up page for any sharp gardener. In the park-like setting of Huntington Botanic Gardens in San Marino, California, sword-like tassles of *Beaucarnea* (syn. *Nolinia*) *recurvata* contrast with ground-hugging echinocactus. These tender plants amply demonstrate the sharp look, which gardeners in temperate climates can aspire to with similar shapes and forms – *Cordyline australis* and santolinas.

Spiky extravagance to provide shelter and create height

At East Ruston Old Vicarage, in north Norfolk, located 3km/1½ miles from the North Sea, effective shelterbelts are a necessity. The old hedges have gradually disappeared from the surrounding fields, but the proximity to the sea means that the garden stays mild. Normally there is no frost before Christmas. Also in the region's favour is a low rainfall of 50cm/20in per year and a free-draining sandy loam. Created by Graham Robeson and Alan Gray since 1986, this garden is a show-case for rare plants which thrive happily in a coastal setting. This is gardening in a grand style, especially in today's terms, when few gardens are being created on such an operatic scale.

In order to garden in their favoured architectural and exotic style it was imperative for the owners to plant shelterbelts of the Monterey pine (*Pinus radiata*), the Italian alder (*Alnus cordata*), *Eucalyptus coccifera*, ash (*Fraxinus excelsior*) and sweet chestnut (*Castanea sativa*). Once these primary shelterbelts began to offer some protection, the possibilities for their style of planting began to open up. Their interests lie in the Mediterranean and the tropical, and they have enthusiastically created a desert wash, complete with agaves, dasylirions, cacti and mature palms, all of which they leave out in winter.

They use phormiums as evergreen shelterbelts to subdivide the garden and these associate well with the wind-tolerant cabbage palm *Cordyline australis*, *Phillyrea angustifolia* and various hollies.

To create a Mediterranean garden here, shelter from trees was not enough: walls had to be built. The resulting extensive amount of brickwork, including both walls and raised beds, gives extra warmth to the plants in winter. Within these Mediterranean borders, phormiums and yuccas are used as accent plants among a profusion of osteospermums, lavender and prostrate rosemary. This area lent itself to this style of planting as it faces south, receiving the maximum amount of winter sunshine. The gravel mulch looks appropriate and helps keep the plants' necks dry.

Gardens do not come much flatter than in Norfolk, so to create height whole avenues have been made with cordylines. Shelter and the mild climate have allowed a couple of cordylines to reach 6m/20ft. In the autumn border, *Phormium tenax* Purpureum Group looks dashing among *Sedum spectabile* and grasses, from tight clumps of miscanthus to the feathery *Pennisteum alopecuroides*. Phormiums make a fine first line of defence against strong winds, especially prevalent in flat gardens and coastal districts.

In the tropical border Graham and Alan use the golden-striped canna, *C.* 'Striata', to great effect, echoing the giant paddle-shaped leaves of the banana palm *Musa basjoo*, whose leaves, because of the adequate shelter, remain untorn by wind.

At East Ruston Old Vicarage in wind-swept north Norfolk, a shelterbelt of the Monterey pine (*Pinus radiata*) is essential to provide protection for *Agave americana* 'Marginata' (top left), *Phormium* 'Yellow Wave' (centre right) and *Yucca filamentosa* 'Bright Edge' (bottom right).

Designing around lush lances in New Zealand

The 4.8 hectare/12 acre countryside garden at Ayrlies, south-east of Auckland City, New Zealand, demonstrates how to create a subtropical effect on heavy coastal clay. Bev McConnell has been gardening here for over forty years. The advantage of the location on a large isthmus is that there is seldom a frost lower than −2°C/28°F, but as well as the high rainfall of over 161mm/50in per annum there are extremes of wind and humidity. The occasional summer drought, sometimes lasting a month, causes cracks in the clay wide enough to take a man's foot. Bev has added drainage wherever possible, and builds up the soil with various mulches, compost and gravel. She designed the garden to include three large recirculating waterfalls – working with the high rainfall and heavy soil. She has developed a subtropical oasis, rich in swords and lances, brightly coloured spires of flowers and a healthy smattering of grasses.

One of the most captivating areas is the rockery, planted forty years ago with a temperate blend of conifers, maples and dwarf bulbs. Over the years an emphasis on subtropical plants has evolved, especially around the swimming pool, owing much to the plantings of agaves, aloes, bromeliads and cycads. Surprisingly, the few remaining maples and dwarf conifers do not jar.

Other areas abound with sharp gardening moments. Recognizing that sword-shaped leaves provide the basis for memorable garden pictures, Bev plants a star performer, echoes it with a spiky supporting plant, and either echoes or softens the scheme with ground cover.

Below her 'sitooterie' (from the Scots, meaning 'a place to sit out in') is a slope planted with lush lances and spiky swords. The tall lance-shaped leaves of *Doryanthes palmeri*, the spear lily, is used as the focal point. Curiously, although it is spiky, the massed foliage of *Agave geminiflora* appears to soften the hard outline of the doryanthes, as this agave's narrow filamental leaves have the effect of grey grasses. The porcupine effect is weighted to the ground by carpet bedding of silvery white rosette-forming *Echeveria elegans*, which Bev enjoys as a most uncomplaining succulent. These echeverias have grown into hefty clumps, from a distance resembling rockery stones. Their silveriness is echoed, and the spikiness softened, by silver-leaved, deep blue *Teucrium fruticans*, a flowering shrub at the top of the bank.

Bev uses this technique again, using different plants to reiterate the theme. She grows the striking sword-shaped *Furcraea gigantea* 'Marginata' as the focal point, with *Aloe camperi* (syn. *A. eru*) as the supporting plant with yellow-orange flowers, growing to about 1m/39in high in summer. These two plants are softened with white marguerite daisies and the lime-green *Helichrysum petiolare* 'Limelight'. The Australian frangipani tree *Hymenosporum flavum* 'Gold Nugget' further softens the picture and adds height.

Where rocky outcrops exist Bev grows smaller, greyer plants. Plain green *Phormium cookianum* with its arching lance-shaped leaves contrasts with shrubby shiny-leaved *Coprosma*

'Yvonne' and *Pimelea prostrata*, which forms a compact grey-green leathery mat beneath the main plants, spreading like the echeverias.

Elsewhere in the garden the combination of perennial *Acanthus spinosus* with the grass *Miscanthus sinensis* 'Morning Light' is a good one, as the narrow white leaf margins of the miscanthus echo the white of the acanthus flowers. In damp areas Bev grows *Carex elata* 'Aurea' with the lance-shaped leaves of the dwarf *Zantedeschia aethiopica* 'Childsiana'. Near water, she uses *Carex secta* and *C. buchananii* with *Chionochloa flavicans*, which is like a small pampas grass. In a large garden these grassy interludes relax the eye after moments of high drama with spiky plants.

Plantings at Ayrlies. **BELOW, LEFT** Lance-leaved *Doryanthes palmeri* with silver-grey rosettes of *Echeveria elegans* in the foreground; grass-like *Agave geminiflora* punctuates the centre. **BELOW, RIGHT** *Furcraea selloa* var. *marginata* dominates here; the red-hot-poker-like flowers of spiny-margined *Aloe* 'Camperi' are softened by *Helichrysum petiolare* 'Limelight' caught by the sun. **FOLLOWING PAGES** Around the swimming pool *Agave attenuata* (right centre), *Cycas revoluta* (foreground) and various aloes burst out of the ground to create a show-stopping scene.

Spiky rosettes

PREVIOUS PAGES *Aloe polyphylla*. **LEFT** The formidable, spiny spikes of *Agave americana* 'Mediopicta', with leaves up to 2m/7ft long.
FOLLOWING PAGES, LEFT, CLOCKWISE FROM TOP LEFT *Agave americana* 'Mediopicta', *A. parryi*, *Beschorneria yuccoides*, *A. victoriae-reginae*.
RIGHT Contrasting agaves: statuesque evergreen 'blooms' of blue-grey *Agave tequilana* is the main plant; *A. striata* (left) adds a grass-like contrast; in the foreground *A. celsii* unfurls its foliage like a rose bud.

Spiky rosettes

More foliage plants to add contrast and complete the skeletal framework

Rosettes of foliage often look like flowers. The unfurling leaves of an *Agave attenuata* resemble a sculptured glaucous rose bud. On close inspection tight clumps of sempervivums or *Aloe aristata* take on the look of weird reptilian dahlias. Like swords and lances, such plants are also linchpins that create the bones of a sharp design. The leaves of most rosettes end in a sharp point and many of them have finely toothed serrations, which continue the sharp theme. Some rosettes – as on most agaves and puyas – are lethally margined with sharks' teeth. Any creature foolish enough to forage among these spines will be barbed as it tries to extricate itself; gardeners' ungloved hands too, briskly clearing out dead leaves caught among the spines, will suffer the same fate.

But although their leaves are sharp, the shape or habit of spiky rosettes is different, so while they continue the theme they also offer further contrasts: they make rounded shapes which complement and offset the horizontals and verticals of spears.

SCULPTURAL ROSETTES

Agaves, from the mountains and deserts of the Americas and West Indies, have naturalized themselves in Mediterranean countries. Although many of these evergreen succulents are monocarpic (they die after flowering), they have a grandeur that is irresistible, and after a plant has flowered so spectacularly, it can be forgiven for dying messily. Fortunately there are always young ones clustering around the base of the dead parent to continue the life cycle.

Agaves grow in a rosette formation. This protects the youngest new shoots in the centre of the plant and creates a natural slope directing any moisture into the heart of the plant to the central stem. The central unopened spear of leaves looks like the enormous beak of some predatory bird; the still-forming teeth of the emerging leaves look as though they belong to an upper and lower jaw. The outer leaves are hard and unyielding, margined with a serrated edge of saw-like teeth. The tips are needle-sharp. As described earlier (see page 20), agaves can take any amount of sun and

need sharply drained soil to be at their best. In southern Spain they grow along the edges of railway lines with the same vigour as buddlejas do in more northern climates. They look incredible growing over cliff-like rocks, like some melting plant in a Dalí painting. Their curling leaves like crab pincers seem to be clutching on to the rock.

The blue-grey *Agave americana* is the best known. A full-grown plant can spread to 2m/7ft tall and be 3m/10ft wide. The flowering spike may reach 8m/25ft high. Old spikes on dead plants make dramatic silhouettes against the sky. It is half hardy (0°C/32°F) to frost tender (5°C/41°F). The glaucous-leaved and yellow-margined *A.a.* 'Marginata' makes a pleasing contrast with the blue-grey agaves. *A.a.* 'Mediopicta' has a central yellow stripe and *A.a.* 'Mediopicta Alba' a central white stripe, but these are frost tender. They look more refined, but are harder to grow in frost-prone areas. Black spots appear on the leaves in winter, usually because of overly damp conditions. If frost attacks them, the seemingly impregnable foliage turns to a mushy pulp. As the plants mature the old basal leaves can be removed and the agave begins to form a squat trunk.

Other highly desirable frost-tender agaves, for warmer climates, include *A. attenuata*, which has pointed, smooth-margined leaves (70cm/28in), with the central bud rising out like a rhino's horn. If you are in an area of high rainfall it is a good idea to grow frost-tender agaves on their sides so that excess moisture runs off the plants and their roots, or just grow them in containers overwintered under glass. *A. victoriae-reginae* makes clumps of white-margined leaves up to 30cm/12in long. *A. stricta* makes a condensed mass of narrow lances up to 35cm/14in long, tapering to a knitting-needle bayonet point. Although classed as frost tender, it tolerates a reasonable UK winter without hardship. The narrow lance-like leaves seem less prone to those black spots caused by damp.

Beschorneria yuccoides looks like a cross between an agave and yucca. It is a perennial succulent classed as a member of the *Agavaceae* family, originating from Mexico's semi-arid regions. It grows in a rosette formation, and its leaves are fleshy and lance-shaped. There is a subtle mottling on the foliage – one way of distinguishing it from a furcraea. The leaves grow to about 50cm/20in, but it is more remarkable for its phallic flower, which emerges as 1.5m/5ft panicles of astonishing red bracts and nodding greeny-yellow flowers on pink stems. Not a plant to linger in front of with teenagers. It is just half hardy (0°C/32°F) and needs a sharply drained spot in full sun. It is best tucked in against a sunny wall and survives in the UK if given the right free-draining conditions. As with agaves, the centre of the plant expires after blooming but emerging babies springing up around the base soon take over, with luck flowering the following year.

Also members of the *Agavaceae* family, furcraeas are perennial succulents from Central America, northern South America and the West Indies. *F. foetida* is classed as frost tender, so needs an almost frost-free climate to survive. Although succulents usually require well-drained poor soil, furcraeas prefer a rich soil. The lance-shaped leaves are glossy and mid-green, with a few small

Trachycarpus fortunei, with yellow flowers and its trunk cleaned of its normal hairs, *Agave americana* (foreground) and grey *Yucca rostrata* on trunks (right). Alliums and grasses make the spiky rosettes look sharper. **FOLLOWING PAGES** An equatorial succulent garden with strong sharp shapes: trunk-forming *Yucca filifera*; blue *Agave americana*, centre-stage; tall spires of the cactus *Marginatocereus marginatus* providing vertical interest in the middle distance; and the grass-like spiny leaves of *Dasylirion longissimum* in the foreground.

teeth found along the bottom third of the leaf. Above this the leaf margin is smooth.

The variegated variety *F.f.* var. *mediopicta* is even more striking, with creamy white longitudinal lines on 2.5m/8ft long leaves. The appeal is heightened because the cream markings are more dominant than the green, so the leaves appear like cream-coloured flames. The leaves are mostly smooth-margined, with a few hooked spines. As furcraeas like sun or partial shade, the cream leaves will add a glamorous touch to a shady corner. Partial shade is a requirement in a hot desert climate, to prevent leaf scorch. Sensationally, in summer, *Furcraea foetida* produces a 6m/20ft flowering stem drenched in strongly scented white flowers.

Spiny-stemmed *Chamaerops humilis* is a half-hardy dwarf fan palm, native to the Mediterranean, where it likes full sun and good drainage. Dwarf in this case means 2–3m/7–10ft tall with a spread of 1–2m/3–7ft. Rather than forming a palm-like trunk *C. humilis* makes a bushy tree, retaining its leaves almost to the ground. The barbed stems, snapping off easily and embedding themselves in the skin, are a good warning to munching predators – and to gardeners pruning dead lower leaves. The dark green circular leaves are pinnate, like a heavily cut Japanese fan. *Chamaerops humilis* is excellent for a small garden. Because of its wide growing habit it lends itself to being a container specimen for a couple of years at least. It's unlikely to get blown over. It associates well with the taller Chusan palm, *Trachycarpus fortunei*. It is a touch less hardy but can withstand short periods of around 0°C/32°F.

The lance-shaped leaves of the cycad, or

LEFT European dwarf fan palm (*Chamaerops humilis*). **RIGHT, TOP** In this north London garden *Chamaerops humilis, Phormium tenax* 'Variegatum' and *Aralia elata* 'Variegata' create a subtropical presence. **RIGHT, BOTTOM** Frost-tender *Cycas revoluta* (left) is just about able to withstand a British winter.

Japanese sago palm, *Cycas revoluta*, grow in a rosette formation. Although not strictly a palm, this plant has a palm-like appearance. From Australia and southern Asia cycads enjoy the arid conditions of the semi-desert and dry, stony slopes. *C. revoluta*, from Japan, has pinnate leaves, usually around 0.75m/30in long, and up to 125 sickle-shaped dark green leaflets. These arching leaves emerging from the stocky trunk give the appearance of a somewhat stunted palm. It is nonetheless attractive and desirable. Although frost tender it is worth trying in sheltered gardens in mild areas.

SCALY ROSETTES

Euphorbia myrsinites comes from southern Europe as far as Turkey and central Asia. Its scaly blue-grey foliage and semi-prostrate habit make it resemble a creeping reptile such as an iguana. The pointed leaves grow in a spiral rosette, and the familiar euphorbia yellow-green flowers spill out at the ends in spring. This foliage looks exactly like the leaves of the monkey puzzle tree – but a different colour and habit, of course. An excellent plant for trailing over rocks and walls, it revels in sun and sharp drainage. It makes only a small plant, 30cm/12in across, so it needs to be used generously to make a splash. *E. myrsinites* is fully hardy. Similar in colour, habit and hardiness, but twice as large, is *E. rigida*. Extending to 60cm/2ft, it flowers from spring into early summer.

Exotic monkey puzzle trees grew to be so popular in Victorian England that they became victims of their own success – popular to the point of nausea and then despised for almost a century. But this is an unjust fate for this hardy evergreen Chilean tree. We can now appreciate the magnificent specimens of *Araucaria araucana* in their glorious maturity. They have the capacity to grow to 25m/80ft with a width of 10m/33ft. Their shape and leaf is like no other. The dark green leaves, which are whorled rosettes and sharply pointed, look like swaying monkeys' tails. Imagine a young tree surrounded by scaly Euphorbia myrsinites.

After these trees' years in the wilderness, designers are now allowing them back into gardens. Even as a young sparsely branched specimen, although without the domed habit of their maturity,

the monkey puzzle tree has plenty to offer. I like the idea of one as a specimen among other spiky plants. Although its overall shape is fuzzy, which creates a contrast, individual leaves are sharp and spiny to the touch. It is difficult to know where to place one, as pruning is impossible as it will ruin the shape; but it is time gardeners with space on their hands began planting these trees in earnest again. They need a moist but well-drained open site, sheltered from cold winds.

SPIKY ROSETTES

The vast armoury of spiky rosettes produce a more arid effect than lush swords and lances. Hard, spiny and lethal to the touch, they look ferocious, but they are a compelling feature of any design. As hard to ignore as diamonds, their assertive spikes shriek attention. These plants make the ultimate focal points.

One of the most rebarbative-looking of the spiky tribe, the evergreen perennial *Aciphylla squarrosa*, resembles a huge steely grey porcupine. A mass of knitting-needle-sharp quills rise from a central crown 90cm/3ft in length. It is also known as the bayonet plant or speargrass. Plant one of these near a path at your peril. Aciphyllas are mostly found in New Zealand, with a few in Australia, in alpine regions, and prefer moist but well-drained conditions. From the stiff unwieldy clump emerges a large spiked stem covered in dull white flowers, the spikes extending beyond the flowers.

Although *Aciphylla squarrosa* looks like a desert inhabitant, it can tolerate the high rainfall of Cumbria. One flowered in my garden for a couple of seasons, once with four flowering spikes, before expiring quietly after an excessively wet winter the year afterwards. It is not supposed to flower in cool climates, so this was a happy surprise. Given plenty of room, and sited carefully where it won't be a potential cause of blindness, it has excellent curiosity value. It must have well-drained but moist soil, preferably with grit added.

Astelia chathamica hails from the southern hemisphere too: this time the Chatham Islands. It is not only sword-like: in the case of *A.c.* 'Silver Spear' it demands inclusion in the sharp garden by its very name. Astelias are evergreen perennials enjoying boggy, peaty soil in mountainous or subalpine areas of Australasia, southern South America, New Guinea and Hawaii.

Astelia chathamica makes a superb architectural specimen. A mature plant resembles a giant silver hedgehog, 1.2m/4ft high with a spread of 2m/7ft. Imagine a mass of 1m/39in long slightly arching, silvery-green leaves, each pleated down the centre and ending in a sharp point. Despite its metallic sun-loving appearance, it prefers partial shade but will take full sun. I have grown it in full sun on poor soil and it has looked none the worse for wear. The silvery sheen draws the eye in the half-light. However, the sunnier the spot the more brightly will the silver gleam. Grow astelias for their foliage. The pale yellowish flowers, 8mm/⅜in across, appearing late in the season, are nothing much.

Astelia nervosa is less glittery. More green than silver, it is more tolerant of semi-shade, and therefore useful as a vertical accent plant where a sun-lover will not flourish. So in a garden with a shady area you could plant it to echo sun-loving spiky plants elsewhere in the garden. The leaves are likely to be shorter than those of *A. chathamica*, at 60cm/2ft, but may extend to 2m/7ft. A twenty-year-old specimen can be 1.8m/6ft in diameter. Both plants should be frost hardy and need only little winter protection. Again well-drained soil is the key. Most silver-leaved plants are intolerant of winter wet and heavy soils, and astelias are no exception. Ideally these astelias should be planted in moist peaty soil (which retains the moisture) in a cool spot, watered liberally in summer, and kept just moist in winter. Again, a raised bed and well-drained soil will do much to ensure the plants' survival.

LEFT *Euphorbia myrsinites.* **ABOVE** The monkey puzzle tree, *Araucaria araucana.*

BARBED ROSETTES

Dasylirion acrotrichum is one of those spiny talking-point plants, with an evergreen fibre-optic lamp silhouette that looks as though it's come straight out of the desert. Its highly serrated finely toothed leaves, about 1m/39in long, emerge from a central rosette. If it flowers for you after a few years the stem will reach a height of almost 4m/12ft, and be covered with tiny bell-shaped flowers throughout most of the summer – an unforgettable sight. It is classed as frost tender but on well-drained soil, the drier the better in winter, it will stand a few degrees of frost. It is well worth trying as, hailing from Mexico and the southern USA, it looks exactly what it is – a perennial succulent from the deserts and dry mountainous areas. Give it what it needs – a sheltered location enjoying lots of sun on well-drained soil – and it should romp. It can be thirsty in summer, so water freely and add a monthly liquid feed if you're feeling impatient.

Puya chilensis is deadly. This evergreen perennial of the bromeliad family has lance-shaped leaves with lethal barbs running down their length. Try groping for some lodged leaves in the centre of a puya and you will find the back of your hand tearing against each spine. In the Andes it is not uncommon for grazing sheep to become fatally attached to the countless barbs. Once trapped the sheep face a grim death by starvation. The leaves of *Puya chilensis*, from central Chile, will reach 1m/39in and if you are lucky it will throw out a 1.5m/5ft flowering stem of yellow or green flowers – an outstanding sight. The 6cm/2½ in waxy flowers hold a cup of rich and syrupy nectar, irresistible for birds and bees. In the right conditions it has the potential to grow 5m/15ft high and 2m/7ft across. The good news is that puyas can survive the cold more than most bromeliads and it helps to plant them in a raised bed to assist drainage. *P. chilensis* is best kept on the dry side in winter; although half hardy it does not appreciate frost after heavy rain and may turn to mush. You can expect a better chance of survival if you initially grow on the plant and repot for a few years, before planting it in spring, preferably against a south-facing wall – patience will pay off. Its natural habitat is on rocky slopes and it is sensible to copy its favoured growing conditions in the garden.

Also from Chile, and growing at an altitude of 400m/1,300ft, are the fascicularias. In a garden setting, fascicularias prefer a sunny well-drained spot, the poorer the better, although they will tolerate partial shade. The enemy is, as usual, winter wet. But in Cumbria and south-west Scotland (with 1m/43in per annum, much of it in winter) they are hardy to −6°C/19°F. Like the puyas, they have barbed spiny foliage, growing in a rosette. *Fascicularia bicolor*, which is the one I have found most reliably hardy, develops a crimson centre among its innermost leaves at flowering time in late summer or early autumn.

LEFT, CLOCKWISE FROM TOP *Astelia chathamica* 'Silver Spear' with agapanthus flowers; *Fascicularia pitcairniifolia* (syn. *F. bicolor*); *Puya chilensis*. **RIGHT** Every *Dasylirion acrotrichum* leaf is margined with tiny teeth.

YUCCAS

Yuccas are the most instantly recognizable spiky plant. Even non-gardeners can spot a yucca a mile off. The dramatic outline of these woody-based perennials is unmistakable, even among other sword-like plants. Yuccas are as tough as their outward appearance suggests. Impervious to neglect once established, they often become permanent fixtures in abandoned gardens. In the once glorious Riviera garden of Lawrence Johnston at Serre de la Madone in Menton, yuccas are the main survivors on the furthest slopes above the villa, among a sea of valerian.

Yuccas originate in North and Central America, and the West Indies. The ultimate architectural perennial succulents (although some are monocarpic), yuccas form rosettes of lance-shaped leaves to create an instantly recognizable structured outline. There are three distinct habits. Some form stemless clumps on the ground; some make a short-stemmed woody trunk; and others develop into sparsely branched 10m/30ft trees.

When trying to recreate an appropriate habitat for yuccas in your garden, remember that the stemless yuccas are usually from the cooler northerly habitats – such as the Great Plains, eastern North American forests and the southerly areas of the Rocky Mountains. Yuccas that form single or multiple trunks are more tropical or subtropical beasts, from the more humid eastern states of the US, or the arid western states and most obviously in the furnace-like Mexico and Guatemala.

Theoretically you could have a garden designed around all three shapes, providing a tree canopy, shrub-level planting and ground cover. The foliage is normally blue-green or dark green. Variegated specimens are more appealing. As well as their rosette-forming foliage, yuccas produce a spire of creamy-white bell-shaped flowers, usually in mid- to late summer. It is not always true that it takes seven years for one to flower, but they do take time to settle down before flowering. Those in the happiest conditions will please you earlier – in only three seasons. Yuccas can take any amount of sun and the more well drained the soil the better.

So you may wish to plant trunkless species on the edge of shadier parts of the garden, as exotic ground cover. If you have an area where you can plant the trunk-forming varieties so that they stand out against the sky, you should find the effect both

ABOVE, TOP *Yucca rostrata*; **ABOVE, BOTTOM** *Agave geminiflora*. Agaves and yuccas can be alarmingly similar – always check the label. **OPPOSITE** Tree-like *Yucca filifera* underplanted with *Furcraea longaeva* (middle and right), *Agave triangularia* 'Jacobi' (left) and *Pactrycereus* (foreground).

dramatic and pleasing. Remember that the plant should look appropriate to the setting.

Living up to its name, *Yucca gloriosa* is one of the best. Its common name is Spanish dagger. The leaves of this particular yucca may reach 50cm/20in long, and as the plant matures it forms a trunk, or several trunks. The trunk is usually naked, so the jagged spears, hard and lethally pointed, starting blue-green and maturing to dark green, and jutting out of the top, look startling. The leaves are matt. In the right spot it may flower in only three years. Rising to a maximum of 2.5m/8ft, the flowering spike is an unforgettable sight. *Y.g.* 'Variegata' is one of my favourite yucca forms, with thick margins of creamy yellow highlighting each dark green leaf, which gives the plant special vibrancy. Yuccas are often sold misnamed, so do not confuse it with *Y. filamentosa* 'Bright Edge' or 'Variegata'. A specimen of *Y.g.* 'Variegata' planted in breathable membrane sheeting in the cool moist climate of Cumbria has flowered at the end of three seasons.

Two of the most readily available ground-hugging yuccas are *Y. filamentosa* and *Y. flaccida*. The dark green leaves of *Y. filamentosa* are margined with spiders' web-like threads. Leaves usually reach 75cm/30in and the flowering spire rises to 2m/7ft. More interesting are the variegated forms: *Y.f.* 'Variegata' has white-margined leaves, and *Y.f.* 'Bright Edge' has a broad margin of yellow that leaves a narrow central line of dark green, yellow being the dominant colour from a distance. *Y. flaccida* is slightly shorter, at 55cm/22in, with a less imposing flowering spire, growing to 1.5m/5ft. The variegated form *Y. flaccida* 'Golden Sword' is yellow margined.

Perhaps the finest of the stemless yuccas is *Y. whipplei*, (known as Our Lord's candle), which has a 2m/6½ft spire of fragrant creamy-white flowers. Unfortunately it usually takes many years to settle down and flower. The leaves are very slender and linear with tiny teeth serrating the edges.

The lance-like leaves of *Y. recurvifolia* extend up to 90cm/3ft long. The plant makes a shrub up to 2.5m/8ft tall, with branches emerging sparsely from the main trunk. The flowering spike reaches 2m/7ft. The leaves are arching, then strongly recurved – hence the name.

Of the tree forms, *Y. aloifolia* is slow-growing, but should eventually make an 8m/25ft tree. The leaves make very narrow toothed lances – it is also known as Spanish bayonet. The white-flowering spikes reach up to 45cm/18in. *Y. aloifolia* is only hardy in temperatures around 7°C/45°F, so is just borderline in a sheltered garden. Winter wet may finish it off.

Y. rostrata also forms a single trunk, to 1.8m/6ft and beyond. The leaves extend to about 0.4m/15in and are very narrow at 1.3cm/½in. The main appeal is the hemispherical head of pale glaucous leaves which make it highly desirable as a focal-point plant among other spiky ornamentals. It should stand temperatures to −15°C/5°F.

Slightly less hardy to −3°C/27°F, *Y. elephantipes* has become one of the most popular houseplants. However, its tree-like habit, reaching up to 10m/30ft, means that it simply grows too large for the average sitting-room. The sight of a fully mature one growing outside, covered in 1m/39in white flowering spikes is unforgettable. The variegated *Y.e.* 'Variegata' has narrow cream-white margins.

GROUND-HUGGING ROSETTES

Sempervivums, or houseleeks, make tight and impregnable rosettes of sharply pointed leaves. Native to European mountainsides, bar one from Morocco, most of them are fully hardy. In the wild they are likely to be blanketed by an insulating carpet of snow which keeps them snug and dry. However, the same rules of sharp drainage to counterbalance wet are most important, as in most gardens there will be no such blanket of snow. The softly hairy species are less able to cope with wet winters and so if in doubt you may need to grow them under glass to ensure their survival. Although one houseleek may look very much like another to the undiscerning eye, there is an enormous variation in their shape, foliage colour and size. Black and purple are always appealing in a garden setting, but there are also ones in yellow and orange, and plain old green and grey. Some of the most eyecatching ones have a fine gossamer film of cobweb hairs stretching from point to point – as with *S. arachnoideum*, for instance, which lives up to its name. It has mid-green to red rosettes up to 2.5cm/1in across, its woolliness contrasting well with the rich purple and black forms. *S.* 'Commander Hay' has side-plate-like rosettes up to 10cm/4in across, comprising lance-shaped glossy deep red-purple leaves. A good dark-tipped spiky one is *S. calcareum* 'Extra'.

Sempervivums are monocarpic (dying after flowering), so it is a good idea to remove each flowering stalk before flowering to promote longevity, if you are not bothered about the flowers. Their drought tolerance makes them ideal container plants, and a finite life cycle makes more space for up-and-coming rosettes, which should allow the plants many years' growth without being repotted. However tantalizing it may look, it makes sense to avoid buying one in bud. On a bank they make a steady-growing succulent carpet with a patchwork effect if you use different colours.

OPPOSITE *Yucca gloriosa.* **BELOW, LEFT** A contemporary treatment for aloes in a San Francisco roof garden container. **BELOW, RIGHT** Drought-tolerant sempervivums make a good low-maintenance choice for a shallow container.

Aeoniums are like sempervivums on stalks. Subshrubby evergreen perennials, their rosettes of fleshy leaves contrast well with the horizontals and verticals of sharp foliage. Hailing from the Canaries, Mediterranean and North African hillsides, they are frost tender. UK winters are normally too wet for them, but daring gardeners might experiment with them as they are borderline candidates for coping with the odd overnight blast of frost if kept dry. However, they are best overwintered under glass to be on the safe side.

One of the most well-known aeoniums is *A. arboreum*, which has a rosette spanning 20cm/8in across with pale green leaves 15cm/6in long making up each rosette. In late spring the plant throws out a panicle of yellow flowers 30cm/12in long. The variety 'Zwartkop' is highly desirable with glossy deep purple leaves which are almost black. In a frost-free area a plant has the potential to make a 2m/7ft subshrub. *A. haworthii* has smaller rosettes and is a more miniature plant at 60cm/2ft. Its bluish green rosettes are desirably sharp, being pointed and toothed.

Aloes are generally frost tender, mostly originating from South Africa and Madagascar, but many will cope with −5°C/23°F. The clump-forming *A. aristata* appears at first sight like a sempervivum, with similarly tight rosettes. As well as being pointed, the lance-shaped leaves are minutely toothed, both along the edges and on the undersides. This is deadliness in miniature. The dark green leaves are white-margined to 10cm/4in long. In autumn cylindrical orange-red flowers appear, no higher than 12cm/5in. This aloe is one of the hardiest and will stand −5°C/23°F.

In cooler climates it is worth being daring with *A. striatula*, which is hardy to −9°C/16°F. The mid-green leaves, up to 30cm/1ft long, growing in a rosette formation, are minutely toothed along the

LEFT At the Abbey Gardens, Tresco, spheres of aeoniums make excellent contrasts with the vertical swords and rosettes in the background. **BELOW** The spherical heads of *Aeonium arboreum* and the deep purple variety 'Atropurpureum' provide evergreen 'blooms' for the sharp garden **FOLLOWING PAGES, LEFT** Finely toothed rosettes on stilts: *Aloe* x *principis* at Huntington Botanic Gardens at San Marino, California. **RIGHT** Not the French Riviera but Morecambe Bay in Cumbria. At Yewbarrow House *Aloe striatula* emerges from behind *Dasylirion acrotrichum*, with fans of *Trachycarpus fortunei* in the background. Scots pine (*Pinus sylvestris*) and yew (*Taxus baccata*) provide a shelterbelt.

ABOVE, LEFT *Celmisia spedenii*, gravelled up to the neck. **ABOVE, RIGHT** In her garden in Dublin, Ireland, Helen Dillon has a separate area for her celmisias. They appear to be marching across a gravelled raised bed like a large family of silver spiders. She grows *Celmisia semicordata* like this because as small plants they need to be grouped to make an impact, while the gravel helps to keep the necks of the plants dry.

edges, branching off a stem reaching approximately 60cm/2ft tall. The flowers are a fierce orange-red, emerging from the centre of the rosette. If planted in a well-drained, sunny position with plenty of grit this aloe can withstand UK winters.

Well known for its healing qualities for insect bites and wounds, frost-tender *Aloe vera*, with its rosettes of lance-shaped toothed grey-green leaves 45cm/18in long erupts in summer with tubular yellow flowers, on branching stems up to 90cm/3ft tall.

Most evergreen silver-leaved plants prefer dry-as-a-bone conditions. Not so with celmisias. As with so many New Zealand plants, they enjoy good drainage and cool, moist conditions – moist as in an area of ample rainfall, not sitting in damp soil, especially in winter, in which case they will rot. Otherwise they are fully hardy. If they dry out they need spraying.

Perennial *Celmisia semicordata* from the cool high-altitude grasslands and moors of South Island, New Zealand, and south-eastern Australia, grows in rosettes of slightly silky, silvery foliage. Its yellow-centred white daisies are better with a darker background; they look bleached against silver. But the evergreen lance-shaped leaf is well worth having, and the flowers are cheerful in early summer. Because the flowering stems are not much taller than 30cm/12in it is best viewed at the edge of a raised bed or alpine rockery, echoing bolder lances. It requires moist, well-drained soil, preferably on the slightly acid soil, in sun or light shade.

Plantago nivalis looks like a miniature celmisia shrouded in cobwebs. It can cope with more intense heat than a celmisia can.

DESIGNING WITH SPIKY ROSETTES

Many of these plants offer the basis for the skeletal framework of a sharp garden. Because of their sharp silhouettes, most of them are best viewed against an open sky, and as their preferred growing conditions require open and sunny areas, they need such spaces to survive. Partnering them with rocks makes much sense: rocks not only make them look more natural in a garden setting but also satisfy all sorts of practical requirements. For frost-tender and half-hardy plants they can provide cover for roots, keeping excess moisture at bay and acting as the ultimate mulch. Rocks on rockeries and terraces also provide much-needed drainage, imperative for survival.

Wherever I have planted *Yucca gloriosa* 'Variegata', it looks spectacular. It looks perfectly at home on a rockery and a planting of a dozen or so will emulate French Riviera plantings of *Yucca elephantipes* 'Variegata'. By planting more than one plant you can achieve an effect that is not only sharp but looks wonderfully self-disciplined and unified.

The constant need for good drainage is important with these yuccas as in wet winters the foliage becomes blackened and may rot off. Around the yuccas I would plant lots of *Euphorbia myrsinites*, a plant made for dripping over stones or around rocks, like a scaly necklace. It is a great partner with the yuccas because the lime-green flowers complement the yellow-margined leaves. In frost the combination of the sparkling glaucous foliage with the yucca leaves is striking.

Because of the more urgent drainage requirements of agaves they are best planted on their sides, and among the yuccas they add a tougher and different texture. The blue of *Agave americana* goes well with the variegated yuccas. Why not plant the colour combination the other way around and have grey yuccas with variegated agaves? If you have the right conditions, yes certainly. In a cool area with high rainfall you need to be confident that the less hardy variegated agaves will survive and continue to look good. Or you can bring them out in the summer as glamorous pot plants.

As a highlight, you might throw in a *Dasylirion acrotrichum*. Its long and narrow, serrated tentacles of pale green leaves, forming a perfect hemisphere, add further contrast of leaf and overall shape. I once kept one in a pot for three years, then, tired of repotting, one spring I decided to take the plunge and plant it outside, where it could please itself if it lived or died. This dasylirion's fight for survival seems well honed, at any rate. If only I had bought three, the effect would have been even stronger. I am sure it helped allowing it to become substantial before planting it.

The European dwarf fan palm, *Chamaerops humilis*, would fit in well with these plants. Its bright green, spiny silhouette of tight fan leaves among the yuccas would be brilliantly exotic – and it would be able to survive. To continue the subtropical theme without planting frost-tender echeverias, you could use sempervivums as ground-hugging cushions between larger spiky plants. They are perfect as a low-maintenance ground cover; once one has flowered and died, its siblings will soon take over the space it has left. The dark-coloured ones are effective near variegated plants.

Coping with sun and shade in Dublin's favourable climate

This garden in Ireland tackles a problem facing many city gardeners: that of creating a unified design while growing plants that are at home in sun or shade.

The mild climate enjoyed by Dublin is perfect for creating the jungle look with lush lances, spiky swords and prickles. If, like garden designer Bernard Hickie, you have a city garden, where the temperature rarely falls below −3°C/26°F, and seldom for prolonged periods, there are many possibilities for growing half-hardy plants. His style of planting also demonstrates that you can have a mature garden in only four years, by planting some mature specimens and interweaving fast-growers into the scheme.

Bernard's west-facing garden is 9m/30ft long and 6m/20ft wide. Consequently he has one long sunny south-facing wall and on the opposite side an equally long shady north-facing wall. As many of the sharp plants he wishes to grow prefer a sunny open site, Bernard's challenge is to unify the garden, using spikies which not only tolerate shade but love it. He believes that the repetition of plants and similar shapes unifies the design, and he has followed this belief to such an extent that he has ended up with a creation that is more LA than Dublin. This is especially apparent on his roof terrace, which is simply planted with three large *Agave americana* in cream pots, *Aloe striatula* and echeverias.

Bernard's key plants for sun and shade are astelias, fascicularias and puyas. On his acid soil the combination of *Astelia chathamica* 'Silver Spear' and *Rosmarinus officinalis* Prostratus Group – the least hardy variant but fine in Dublin – is one of his favourites. The contrast of the brushed chrome of the astelia with the dark green rosemary foliage and the deep blue flowers is exquisite.

On the sunny south wall he gets to grips with plants that he can repeat on the shady side. So as well as astelias, he grows *Puya chilensis*, *P. berteroana* and *Fascicularia pitcairniifolia* (syn. *F. bicolor*), which grow at ground level. This last plant laps up the most inhospitable and unkind conditions. He uses *Phormium tenax* soaring above as a focal point, enjoying it for the way its leaves fan out from the base. Bernard steers pretty well clear of variegated plants, but uses *Phormium tenax* 'Variegatum' to echo the shape of the grey-green phormium and inject some creamy yellow among the greys and silvers.

Bernard likes to contrast different plant shapes – spiky, spherical and shrubby with a fuzzy outline – when creating a design. Here he has the spikes of *Puya berteroana*, *Beschorneria yuccoides* and the fat round faces of aeoniums, with a backdrop of the honey-scented *Euphorbia mellifera* and *Melianthus major*. In many gardens *M. major* is best cut to the ground after winter frosts, but Bernard prefers to leave it uncut, merely removing the most ragged leaves from the base and allowing it to form a woody trunk that grows to tree-like proportions of 3m/10ft. Its serrated leaves echo the spikes of the astelias, puyas and fascicularias below, but the

general softness of the plant soothes the eye. To add flowers, as well as the beschornerias he uses the pure-white-flowering *Zantedeschia aethiopica* 'Crowborough' for its simplicity.

On the shady wall opposite he uses some well-known shade-tolerant plants such as big-leaved *Fatsia japonica* and *Eriobotrya japonica*, plus a stand of *Phyllostachys nigra*, all of which act as antidotes to the spiky planting. A massive *Fascicularia bicolor* – 2m/7ft x 1m/39in – is a good plant for spreading over a retaining wall and ascelias are happy in the partial shade. At the furthest end from the house the shade becomes less of a problem and the west end of the garden enjoys much sun, so he is able to grow another *Euphorbia mellifera*, poking its head into the light, and, at the far end, more astelias, beschornerias and agaves.

PREVIOUS PAGE The Chusan palm, *Trachycarpus fortunei*, frames the view of this long narrow Dublin garden, which offers the right degree of shelter and a mild climate. **OPPOSITE** Spikes and spears punctuate Bernard Hickie's designs. **BELOW, LEFT** Barbed rosettes of foliage on a *Puya chilensis*. **BELOW, RIGHT** Bernard Hickie's split-level garden gives him raised beds on which to grow *Aloe striatula* and the blue spires of *Echium pininana*, the verticals thrown into relief by horizontal tree fern fronds.

Low rainfall sharp seaside gardening

In coastal east Essex garden designer Paul Spracklin experiments successfully with many spiky plants. He has two key areas of interest. One has a lush jungly look involving rain-loving exotic plants supported by heavy doses of compost. The other has an arid desert look, and concentrates on spiky plants that hate winter wet, requiring fast drainage and virtually no soil.

Although the average winter temperature is −5°C/23°F, which allows him to grow frost-hardy but not necessarily half-hardy plants, and the rainfall is low for the UK at 500mm/20in, the clay loam soil is not ideal for growing succulents that prefer to be parched. But in his favour he has a south-facing slope with a gradient of one in five. To make the desert-style planting scheme work he decided to change the soil. He capitalized on the steep slope, creating raised beds in a terrace arrangement by moving the edge forward and backfilling with free-draining clinker and sharp grit. Certainly growing the desert-type plants 'hard' gives them a better chance of survival in winter.

This well-drained soil allows him to try his hand with rosette-forming succulents such as agaves, aloes, yuccas, puyas and fascicularias. He contrasts the spikes of rosette-forming succulents with the rounded spiny club-like heads of opuntias, which works well. Much of his work has been trial and error, as there has been no real precedent for growing succulents en masse as landscape subjects, apart from a few people here and there growing the odd opuntia.

Paul has designed a scheme around his succulent plants using evergreen plants. He has chosen star plants and supporting plants and added detail with ground cover. Here, the ground cover is somewhat unconventional, as smaller plants fill the gaps between larger specimens, while echoing the dry spiky succulent theme. Various lava-like rocks give the illusion of a setting in a volcanic Canary Island.

When it comes to feeding his exotic plants, Paul swears by an all-purpose fertilizer such as Vitax Q4, but is sparing with it. He never gives them extra water, except maybe occasionally for the palms. As well as the sharp drainage he maintains that good air circulation is critical, so his succulent bank is located near the top of the garden where, inevitably, it is more open. Conversely, he has placed the moisture-loving exotics in the dip at the bottom of the garden.

RIGHT, TOP Uphill on the succulent bank in Paul Spracklin's tropical garden are a selection of palms, agaves, aloes, puyas, *Echium pininana* and cacti. Downhill the large banana *Musa basjoo* marks the beginning of the jungle garden. Bisecting the two is a series of ponds bridged by decking platforms. In the water *Thalia geniculata* is surrounded by the parrot's feather, *Myriophyllum aquaticum*. RIGHT, BOTTOM RIGHT Mexico in miniature: a mix of desert plants give an arid feel to this area. They relish the drought of an Essex summer and are hardy enough to cope with the winter. RIGHT, BOTTOM LEFT Vicious spikes of palms and succulents, including a silvery blue form of *Dasylirion wheeleri* and the silver fan palm, *Trithrinax campestris*, on the main south-facing bank.

Urban riviera planting

In south-east London, Jason Payne is putting the finishing touches to a garden in which he attempts to take the spiky look possibly as far as you can go in the UK. By building a raised bed, backfilled with as much free-draining material as possible, he has created an environment in which his client can indulge his love of Mediterranean plants, many of which happen to be rosette-forming. The bed is contained by a dry-stone wall of Derbyshire sandstone and the soil surface is mulched with a pea gravel, which focuses the arid theme. Although Jason uses plants discussed in previous chapters such as *Trachycarpus fortunei* and phormiums, his design is rigidly single-minded, using mainly plants of desert origins with the Mediterranean ones.

The garden owes its exotic appearance to a disciplined use of many of the key species outlined above. Agaves and yuccas are the predominant plants. He has repeated *Agave americana* and its yellow-margined variegated form *A. americana* 'Marginata'. The blue-grey or variegated leaves catch the eye immediately, so can be described as the focal-point plants. The more uniform greys of various yuccas develop the main spiky backbone of the scheme. *Yucca*

In Jason Payne's design in a London garden: **LEFT, TOP** *Agave americana* 'Marginata'. **BOTTOM** A palm lurks amid protective bamboo. **RIGHT** Although requiring a raised bed this profusion of exotics shows what can be achieved to mirror the cacti and succulent gardens of abroad. Taking a bow, from the front, are *Aloe striatula*, *Agave americana*, *Yucca whipplei* and *Y. rostrata*, while kniphofia and *Phormium tenax* Purpureum Group add ballast at the rear.

rigida, Y. filifera, Y. whipplei and *Y. glauca* make up this chorus. Then to create a little height Jason has used the trunk-forming *Y. rostrata*, a favourite plant, and *Cycas revoluta*, again trunk-forming, and from a distance forming the same outline.

Garden designer Declan Buckley's plot in Islington demonstrates how effectively sharp gardening works in an enclosed urban space. This is the lush side of sharp gardening as opposed to the desert look. His walled north London garden, measuring 22m/72ft x 6m/20ft, reveals how you can rid your location of the traditional pocket-handkerchief lawn with narrow borders cowering on the perimeters. He replaces the lawn with borders that break up the garden, which is further divided by a jungly overlay, using large out-of-scale plants. Specimens such as bamboos, once regarded as being suitable only for large gardens, make instantly established room-dividers. Their fuzzy outline provides a good foil against which to show off spikes and swords, many of them New Zealand favourites, which embellish this evergreen framework. Declan's influences include his southern Ireland upbringing – where tender exotics enjoy the Gulf Stream influence – plus a stint in California and numerous trips to North Vietnam, Bali and Sri Lanka.

Faced with a long, narrow plot Declan has created an optical illusion of increased width by running a pond across the width of the garden, about a quarter of the way down from the house. You step across this, over a weathered plank bridge, into a jungle beyond. After the rectilinear lines of this area, the mood becomes more relaxed with a gently winding path of

Glossy-leaved *Iris confusa* (above table) works well in urban shade and echoes the phormium's foliage (back centre).

blue-grey slate chippings leading you into Declan's take on the Far East.

Knowing that some of his plants, such as the bamboos, bananas, cannas and hedychiums, are all greedy feeders, he improved the acid-to-neutral loamy soil with lots of manure to give them a good start. He tops this up every other year on the plants that need it. Ironically the nightmare of rubble inevitable in city gardens provided the required free drainage.

This garden is absorbing for the sharp gardener on two counts. Firstly it shows what can be achieved in a long, narrow walled plot with no access except through the house. Declan's style of planting is well suited to this lack of access, for he is not faced with huge amounts of woody growth to clear every year, and he has a compost area hidden at the furthest end of the garden. Using a few large specimens – some of which came from his previous home where he roof-gardened – he created the feeling of a mature garden in only two summers. Now that the garden is five years old it is time to let in more light by raising the crowns on certain trees and shrubs. By cleaning off the trunks he has also created more planting space at ground-cover level.

Secondly Declan demonstrates how this style of planting copes with shade. Although this narrow east-facing garden enjoys a long sunny wall, it also has an equally long shady wall, so he has to use plants that will unify the garden, tolerating both sun and shade.

He is keen on both *Astelia chathamica* and *A. nervosa*, which, fortunately, will thrive in these two extremes. In a London garden the bright silver sheen of *A. chathamica* reflecting light is most welcome, as it gleams even in partial shade. But, just as if you had two bossy relatives with the same characteristics, but preferred one

to the other, *A. nervosa* comes over as the more restful of the pair. *A. chathamica* bursts out of the ground in the same way as *P. tenax*, so it is not restful-looking. *A. nervosa*, although not as glamorously silver, has the more elegant arching leaves, as *P. cookianum*. As the two astelias are planted next to each other here, it is easy to see which one you like more.

In a bed cut into the terrace less than 1m/39in square, Declan demonstrates what can only be described as text-book sharp gardening practice. He likes planting the jet-black *Ophiopogon planiscapus* 'Nigrescens' underneath the astelias, and it looks as though it is going to creep out and dart across the flags like some evil-looking spider. Eucomis provide flowering interest and the pointed leaves tie in with the astelias and ophiopogon.

He picks up the black theme in a nearby border with *Phormium tenax* 'Platt's Black' and purple cannas. The matt-black canna foliage offers a further contrast with these glossy-leaved plants. Other phormiums are represented in this garden, including a 2m/7ft tall *P. tenax*, stretching up for the light, and a couple of containerized *P. cookianum* plants which stand as guards of honour at the far end of the garden. Declan also likes stuffing in fasciularias, such as *F. pitcairniifolia*, which look happy in awkward shady places. With their finely cut spiny leaves they are more arresting than the astelias and phormiums, and as, for the present at least, they take up less space than those plants they are useful punctuation marks on corners and at joints in the garden, where space is at a premium.

Another important plant which unifies this garden is the Chusan palm, *Trachycarpus fortunei*, whose shiny leaves are echoed at a lower level by the impossibly glossy *Fatsia japonica*, making a 1m/39in high shrub, perfectly happy hugging the north wall. As this palm is tolerant of sun and shade, and becomes a dominant feature in any planting, two or three of these dotted on the north and south sides create an instant subtropical atmosphere. He echoes this palm at a lower level at waist height, with the smaller *Trachycarpus wagnerianus* and *Chamaerops humilis* and their fan leaves continue to unify the garden.

It's important to consider what will grow underneath large spiky specimens, especially when the planting fills out and shade becomes more dominant. Even though the crowns on evergreen trees have been raised, there is still shade in the garden – from the wall, from the trees and from the bamboos that have been used to compartmentalize it.

Down in the depths Declan favours *Iris confusa*, which, with its strong leaf shape, makes a good corner plant, especially as it can be rejuvenated by being cut back in late spring to stop it becoming leggy, so it is unlikely to get too large on a strategic corner. In late winter it still looks healthy (by early spring some frost-hardy evergreen plants look as if they are waking up on the wrong side of bed) and in mid-spring the white and yellow flowers show up well. He also uses summer-flowering *Acanthus mollis* in dark corners. It does the job well – you can't have too many glossy plants in a city garden, many of which deteriorate into looking dusty in summer. Strap-leaved *Dianella tasmanica* is another useful evergreen shade-tolerant plant because its long-lasting dark blue berries create interest for many months. Near the house Declan has tucked in *Zantedeschia aethiopica* 'Crowborough' in the shade of a

Drought-tolerant succulents are perfectly happy when congested in containers.

towering banana, *Musa basjoo*, and a couple of tree ferns. The zantedeschia looks right under the banana, and still flowers in partial shade.

Skeletal *Pseudopanax crassifolius*, fast becoming a hot favourite with designers and gardeners, contrasts with the fleshy astelias.

The generous windowsills on Declan's late-Victorian house lend themselves to window boxes, but not of the traditional variety. It would be perverse to have a garden like this and have window boxes filled with scarlet pelargoniums and blue lobelia. He opts instead for galvanized metal troughs filled with succulents which thrive on neglect. Spiny-margined *Aloe striatula* copes well with this kind of life: being impoverished, hungry, thirsty and overcrowded suits it down to the ground. Piled in with a host of other succulents, some unnamed and collected from abroad, it leans out of the trough like a drunken jack-in-the-box. The troughs offer a sharp garden in miniature and are a good way of tying in the house and garden.

Desert planting

In the Ruth Bancroft Garden in Walnut Creek, near San Francisco, California, desert plants, including aloes, agaves, echeverias and yuccas, jostle together like weird reptiles. More than 2,000 species of native plants from dry-land habitats across the globe tumble over each other in these remarkable 1.6 hectares/4 acres. The garden was created through the enthusiasm of owner Ruth Bancroft only in the early 1970s. The present owner's design comprises rounded, raised beds through which paths meander, allowing the visitor to view plants with ease from all sides. The demonstration here of the beauty of spiky plants and their great diversity of texture, scale

and shape has few rivals. Flowers are a bonus in an overall effect of grey-greens and soft blues.

With an annual rainfall of 50cm/20in, most of which falls during winter, and winter temperatures occasionally as low as −7°C/20°F, the ground has been prepared to create acceptable drainage levels. The earth here is clay and hard-panned soil − not the most promising soil for gardening with succulents. Most of the beds are raised from between 30cm/12in to 90cm/36in, which lifts the roots and protects them from waterlogging, which would prove fatal in cold conditions. If you have clay soil, the best time to create a new bed is in spring, when the clay is not heavy with winter wet, or dry and bone hard as it is in summer. A plant has a better chance of survival if planted in spring, with a full season's growth ahead of it before winter sets in.

When a new border is made, the clay earth is dug over and roughly equal amounts of sand, pumice, pebbles and expanded shale are worked in. The border is then mulched with rocks and pebbles, which helps to unify the garden as the paths are made of crushed stone. This vital preparation work in the borders helps to ensure that the garden's desert plants have the best chance of survival. Even so, frost-tender aloes have been killed in adverse weather conditions of −7°C/20°F. This style of planting can never be treated complacently.

A large estate garden such as this affords plenty of opportunities for planting large species of agave, such as pale grey-blue *A. franzosinii* which can reach 3m/10ft tall with a width of 4.6m/15ft, and which demands a large area to be seen at its best. Related to *A. americana*, this plant forms plenty of offsets. The unfurling foliage reveals the imprinted serrated toothmarks of the previously opened leaves.

Yucca filifera is eyecatching here too, as not only is it one of the largest yuccas available, but it has unusual pendent inflorescences. There is also an exceptional specimen of *Y. rostrata* here, planted in 1972. It now has forty or so heads on it – an outstanding sight. *Y. rostrata*'s blue foliage makes a highly ornamental neat grass skirt about itself; it would be a sin to remove it.

So here is a place to inspire any student of spiky plants; and the space to give a home to large specimens. If you want to replicate the atmosphere in your own garden you will have to choose miniature versions of these giants. *Yucca thompsoniana* is a good choice, as its leaves are shorter than *Y. rostrata* (maximum 45cm/18in) and it is equally drought- and cold-tolerant. The stemless yuccas such as *Y. rupicola*, *Y. pallida* and *Y. glauca* are all worth considering.

There are smaller relatives of *Agave americana*, more appropriate in a small area. *A. lourneyana* is an easy plant to cultivate with leaves up to 30cm/12in long. *A. parviflora* is smaller and more compact with leaves only 10cm/4in long. It is a good choice for planting in a container as it will not get too large and unwieldy. It is also worth seeking out *A. polianthiflora* as the only species similar to *A. parviflora* in size and appearance.

If you want the spiky look without sharp spikes try another small species, *A. bracteosa*, whose leaves rarely exceed 30cm/12in. Because of its size and lack of terminal spines it again makes a good choice for container growing. Unusually in agaves this plant is polycarpic, blooming many times in its life without dying.

When choosing agaves here a prime consideration is whether the plant produces offsets. This determines how much space it will take up. In the Californian climate some agaves sucker more than others.

At the Ruth Bancroft Garden, California. **LEFT** *Agave americana* 'Mediopicta Alba' and the swaying spires of Our Lord's candle, *Yucca whipplei*, which can be echoed in temperate gardens by hardier plants with similar flowers. **BELOW** *Yucca rostrata* complete with grass skirt hiding its sturdy trunk.

Spiky flowers, spires & straps

PREVIOUS PAGES Teasel close-up: *Dipsacus fullonum*.
LEFT A spire such as this *Agave filifera* in full bloom
is the inspiration for planting spires of flowers that
echo its shape and stature.

Spiky flowers, spires & straps

Three kinds of flowering perennial to embroider the look

Once you have created a structure of sharp foliage and spiky accents, it's time to decorate.

For some gardeners the plant shapes and foliage of swords, lances and spiky rosettes are enough, and for a low-maintenance garden with few flowers this look is hard to beat; but most gardeners are keen to incorporate flowers into their planting schemes. Flowers are the lifeblood of the garden. After all, they open up so many different seasonal excitements, from the anticipation of emerging buds to fleeting blossom, followed by autumnal seedheads, and finally winter skeletons. Butterflies and insects are part and parcel too, as are birds foraging in them for insects and the food from seedheads. All this creates life and movement, without which no garden is complete; sterility is kept at bay. If nothing else, gardens are about reproduction.

When designing with perennials, it's important to get the backbone right first; I would not plant perennials first and spiky evergreens afterwards. Establish a framework of spiky plants first. Follow this up by adding flowering plants as ornamentals. Just as an artist sketches out the bare bones of the painting first, before adding colours and hues, follow the initial structural planting with bulbs and perennials whose dominant characteristic is flowers, and which complement the colours and textures.

Ignore traditional herbaceous flowers. Perennials such as hostas or hardy geraniums look out of place next to the more hard-living and rugged spiky plants. They may also do damage. Most of the lance-shaped plants and spiky rosettes need to have air circulating around their necks, especially in winter. Perennials with lush foliage, which create a thick eiderdown of leaves, will have a detrimental effect, especially from autumn onwards when the leaves are reduced to a soggy pulp. In summer their foliage will create undesirable shade close to the swords and spikes.

There are other homes for these plants. Besides, their required growing conditions are incompatible. Whereas many herbaceous perennials hibernate and are impervious to winter wet if they are fully or frost hardy, and are happy in moist semi-shade, most sharp foliage plants need sharp drainage, preferring a warm, sunny, well-drained spot. A yucca will not take kindly to a wet winter without good drainage, and may well rot off and even die.

Instead of planting herbaceous perennials, dramatize with spiny flowers, especially those that are prickly to the touch. Ignite with sky-piercing spires that echo the giant blooms of succulents. Finally splash in some contrast with chunky-headed globe flowers whose strap-like leaves echo sharp architectural foliage. By keeping to a smaller palate of perennials with bristling flowers and jagged foliage you will be well on the way to creating the sharp garden look. Narrow the field to those that look appropriate with sword-like foliage, and then have fun playing around with various combinations.

There are three main flower types that fit in with this theme. Barbed, prickly thistle-type flowers such as eryngiums look sharp and are sharp. Tall spires, such as kniphofias, echiums and eremurus, echo the jagged shapes of spiky evergreens. They act as exclamations and have an appealing punchiness. Globe flowers with strappy leaves, such as alliums and agapanthus, rest the eye, acting as full stops. The long narrow leaves are supporting players to lance-shaped foliage. Many of the ones selected here flower from mid to late summer, some well into autumn, so they are valuable for keeping the garden going throughout those late months.

Whereas the foliage on spiky succulents is usually of primary interest, and the flowers are subordinate, most of the leaves on these perennials are subordinate to the flowers and usually echo architectural foliage. Some plants begin life with strap-like leaves, which echo larger lances and swords, but die off leaving the flower as the star attraction, such as alliums.

BARBED, PRICKLY THISTLE-TYPE FLOWERS

If you look at the flowers of many spiky-leaved perennials or better still, touch them gently, you will find that there are hundreds of miniature prickles on each flowerhead. These thistles are low maintenance because they love poor, well-drained soil and full sun, so no lugging and spreading of compost is required. Their survival is threatened by excessive winter wet and shade.

The cardoon thistle, *Cynara cardunculus*, from the Mediterranean and Morocco, is a statuesque perennial, with silver acanthus-like leaves, 50cm/20in long. Looking resplendent in late spring and early summer, its leaves look good enough to eat. You could remove the budding stems if you wanted to enjoy the foliage alone, but it seems a pity to miss its 1.5m/5ft flowering stems with hard spiny flowers topped with a peacock's purple crown. These thistle tips are soft to the touch, like shaving brushes, but beware the spiny barbs that guard them. This sun-loving thistle is best grown out of strong winds, to stop it toppling over, and to perform best needs well-drained fertile soil.

Tall perennials such as *Cynara cardunculus* are plants for the main border. The evergreen silvery foliage starts growing early in spring and is attractive throughout the season. The length and

TOP The spiky flowers of the musk thistle, *Carduus nutans*. **BOTTOM** The RHS Hyde Hall garden in Essex. From the left: *Bergenia* 'Bressingham Ruby', *Phlomis fruticosa*, *Digitalis lutea*, *Verbascum olympicum*, *Euphorbia polychroma* 'Major', *Eryngium bourgatii*, *Agapanthus campanulatus* 'Cobalt Blue', *Helleborus argutifolius*, *Santolina pinnata*, *Stipa tenuissima*.

fleshiness of the foliage mean that it may smother a plant that needs plenty of air around it, which you do not want. Although a young plant does not want to be suffocated, once phormiums are established they are less fussy about this. So plant it near a *Phormium tenax*, where the grey-green of the phormium's foliage is highlighted by the silvery grey cardoon leaves. The size and stature of both perennials are in keeping with each other. You could also place *Cynara cardunculus* in the middle or behind some of the *Phormium cookianum* hybrids. As both have arching leaves they look elegant together.

A very similar-looking thistle is the biennial *Onopordum acanthium* from the Mediterranean, Europe and western Asia. Its grey woolly leaves are spiny-toothed, and at first glance there is not much to distinguish it from the cardoon. How do you tell the difference between the two? Whereas the cardoon flowers on tall stems emerging from the base, the onopordum has side shoots, throwing out from the main stem flowering stems with bright purple thistles. It can reach 2.5m/8ft, in its second and final season. The cardoon is more stately than the onopordum. The onopordum is something of an upstart, self-seeding easily. This can be a curse, but it's easy enough to hoe the seedlings out. Its ability to self-seed makes it a good plant for planting in gravel. If it lands near the front of a border, leave it, because you can look through the freely branching stems to plants behind it. This is a good way of creating perspective.

While the cardoon takes time to settle down, sometimes not flowering until its third season, the biennial onopordum provides flowers within a couple of seasons, so if you are in a hurry you could plant some onopordums while awaiting developments from the cardoons. As with most silvery-leaved plants, onopordum enjoys poor soil and full sun – its preferred habitat is a stony slope. Bear in mind that it needs to be in a border at least 2m/7ft deep so as not to look out of proportion. Bees love onopordum flowers. Once flowering is over the heads turn to cotton down – a reminder that the plant is also called cotton thistle. Its brief life and roving nature add excitement to the garden, for no border will be quite the same the following year, as the onopordums die and settle elsewhere.

Another biennial thistle, *Silybum marianum* (Blessed Mary's thistle), grows to about 1.5m/5ft. Living hard on stony slopes in south-western Europe and north Africa, it prefers full sun and poor, well-drained soil (neutral to slightly alkaline), which help it survive winter wet, although it is fully hardy. With its exaggerated elongated bracts, surrounding purple-pink flowers, it resembles a cartoon version of the cardoon. The foliage is glorious. Marbled with white veins, the glossy dark green leaves are deeply lobed and spiny. Some gardeners remove the flowers to retain silybums as foliage

RIGHT A rose among thorns. **FAR RIGHT** The leaf and flower of *Silybum marianum* have the last word on barbs and prickles.

plants. Incredibly the unpalatable-looking leaves prove delectable to slugs and snails.

Further members of the thistle family include echinops, which reaches 90cm/3ft in height, thriving in dry grassland and sunny gravelly slopes from Europe to Asia, India and the mountainous regions of tropical Africa. Its spiny foliage is grey with white undersides. The globe thistle flowers are a perfect sphere of blue pin-pricks, the colour lasting for several weeks. If you don't cut down the stems in winter you will encourage bullfinches into the garden, hungry for the seeds. Echinops will self-seed if not dead-headed. Look out for the late summer blooms of *Echinops ritro* 'Veitch's Blue', which is a deeper blue than most.

Not only do echinops' pompon flowers contrast well with their leaves, but the spheres make a useful foil for any sword-like foliage. Because they clump up vigorously after three years, it is best to keep them in check by dividing them every couple of years or so, before they encroach on the evergreen leaves of spiky plants. They love poor soil in full sun, and will still flower in partial shade.

Eryngiums are thistles with attitude. Everything about them looks hostile and uninviting. Barbs, spines and prickles sharpen every leaf, bract and flower. Their armoury discourages nibbling herbivores in their native rocky, coastal habitats of Europe, Africa, Asia and China. But in spite of all their repellent protection, they are plants of great beauty. Their umbel flowers are held among the bracts like diamonds in a ring.

Nevertheless, you are unlikely to forget an encounter with a sea holly (*E. maritimum*) if you accidentally stumble upon one barefoot in a sand dune on a seaside holiday. Each leaf is a mass of thorns ready to trap the unwary, and the hard, steely flowers are just as antisocial. The thimble flowers within the bracts are as sharp to the touch as the leaves, but it is the prickly bracts surrounding them that discourage any potential munching predators. Looking so spiny, it is easy to

imagine that these prickly flowers have emerged from the dagger-like foliage of yuccas as if they are yucca flowers themselves. With both plants requiring the same dry, well-drained conditions and full sun, they certainly make good companions.

Confusingly, while many eryngiums prefer these hard growing conditions, others like moist, well-drained and fertile soil, still in full sun. The Argentinian frost-hardy *E. agavifolium* is one such plant, the flowers of which resemble giant thimbles set in small bracts. They lack the blue steeliness of most eryngiums, and are best described as greenish

LEFT Spheres, horizontals and verticals: the thin bands of *Cortaderia selloana* make an airy foil for these prickly *Echinops bannaticus* globes, with a background of *Phormium tenax* 'Variegatum' at Yewbarrow House, Grange-over-Sands, Cumbria. **RIGHT** Sharper than a serpent's tooth: the heavily veined bracts of sea holly *Eryngium maritimum*.

white flowers 5cm/2in long. Reaching well over 1m/39in tall, they stand up well without staking. They come into their own when they turn a deep dark brown lasting all winter – looking much better like this than when flowering in summer. The reference to agaves in their name describes the leaves, which are highly sharp-toothed swords.

There is an eryngium for every location: ranging from gigantic to dwarf there are over 200 species. Here is a handful. Unless otherwise indicated you are safe planting the following in full sun, on poor, dry, well-drained soil.

E. bourgatii, found in the Spanish Pyrenees, bears branching stems with masses of small grey-green flowers, amid star-like silvery blue bracts. The blue stems grow to about 45cm/18in tall. Twice as high, Mediterranean *E.* x *tripartitum* has violet-blue flowers with blue-grey lance-shaped bracts. A good eryngium for a raised bed or rock garden, where the soil does not get too dry, is the Moroccan *E. variifolium*, which reaches 30cm/12in. The silvery white bracts are narrow and pointed, the flower pale blue.

E. giganteum or Miss Willmott's Ghost is an essential biennial, or short-lived perennial, found growing from the Caucasus to Iran. Its highly veined pale green bracts turn to silvery grey and encase steely blue flowers. The whole plant is about 90cm/3ft tall with a spread of 30cm/12in, and seems to look better with age. 'Silver Ghost' is smaller, and more silvery white.

Of particular interest to the sharp gardener are two slightly more tender species: the frost-hardy *E. pandanifolium*, found from Brazil to Argentina, which likes moister, more fertile conditions, and Mexican *E. proteiflorum*. The first should appeal because of its 1–2m/3–7ft-long sword-shaped leaves. The flowering stems can reach 4m/13ft – a magnificent sight. The flowers are less distinguished – a purplish brown – but the leaf and height are outstanding. *E. proteiflorum* has the finest flowers of all, resembling the flowers of protea, the much loved South African shrub from which it takes its name. The leaves are spinily margined and the whole plant reaches 90cm/3ft tall.

LEFT, TOP TO BOTTOM *Eryngium agavifolium*; *E. eburneum*; *E. giganteum*.
RIGHT Deep blue *Eryngium bourgatii* set off by gravel in the Dry Garden at RHS Hyde Hall, Essex. A silhouette of *Cynara cardunculus* echoes the thistle theme.

The prickly common teasel, *Dipsacus fullonum*, from Europe and Asia, is a useful biennial self-seeder in a new garden, until you become tired of it or your garden has filled out sufficiently. It is almost too successful a colonizer: scattering its progeny liberally, it becomes a weed in a few seasons. However, it is useful in an informal area, adding height in the second season as it rises to almost 2m/7ft itself. The airy, sparsely branched habit adds a lightness of touch among heavier, strappier foliage. Bristling purple thistle-like cones encased in rigid, spiny bracts wave above thorny stems. It can be preserved indefinitely if harvested for drying indoors. Alternatively leave it outside, where its ghostly silhouette will look good all winter, especially if rimed with frost.

SPIRES OF FLOWERS

Spires of inflorescences are reminiscent of the thrusting foxtail spikes of many succulents. Individual flowers of these may be a spiny barb or a sharply toothed bract – just the right ingredients for scattering among sword-like foliage.

One of the most architectural of perennials is the acanthus. The name derives from the Greek, *akanthos*, meaning prickle. It normally takes two or three years to flower, as it has to push down a long tap root, but it's worth waiting for. *A. spinosus*, from rocky and dry locations in the Mediterranean, will flower in partial shade as well as full sun. The leaves of *A. mollis* are not so finely cut, but if you want bold foliage they are perfect. Once *A. spinosus* has developed its tap root it throws out a lupin-like spire of spiny bracts to perhaps 1.2m/4ft. The glossy dark green leaves appear as pinnate, more because of their being heavily cut to the midribs than because they are divided. A cluster of small leaves at the base of the plant will stay evergreen through the winter.

Acanthus are useful for planting in partial shade as the leaves always come up trumps, their glossiness much appreciated in the half-gloom, and once the plant has put down its tap root it usually flowers even if the circumstances it finds itself in are unpromising.

An acanthus spire is made up of alternating white and purple two-lipped flowers – resembling a less intricate snapdragon. If you leave the heads on it will stand up for several more weeks,

LEFT *Dipsacus fullonum*, the common teasel. **FOLLOWING PAGES, LEFT TO RIGHT** *Dyckia tuberosa* var. *tuberosa*; *Wachendorfia thyrsiflora*; *Acanthus mollis*.

until the seeds that have formed inside each flower have popped out; the flower husks eventually disintegrate once winter starts to bite. Acanthus is a good-value perennial, in that it earns its keep in the border on each of its merits alone: architectural leaf, long flowering season and versatility as to location. However, acanthus are not everyone's cup of tea, so decide whether you find the low-key purple-and-white combination subtle or funereal. Once planted, an acanthus is difficult to eradicate if you have a change of heart, as even a fragment of the tenacious tap root will develop into a new plant.

With its lance-shaped, glossy and spiny-toothed leaf, the evergreen perennial *Morina longifolia* is similar to acanthus. Its 90cm/3ft spike is covered with waxy white flowers that appear above whorled clusters of spiny bracts; its common name is whorlflower. After they have been fertilized the flowers change colour to rose-pink, then red. This is not a plant that can endure winter wet, one of its native habitats being Himalayan rocky and grassy slopes, so give it a sunny spot in poor, well-drained soil and don't try it in shade. In spite of its spiny leaves, slugs will make inroads if given half a chance. Perhaps they like a challenge.

The biennial *Echium pininana* erupts into a jaw-dropping 4m/13ft flowering spire of hundreds of tiny blue flowers. The sight of a host of these in flower will make other gardeners immediately covetous. This is a Canary Island echium, frost hardy to −5°C/23°F. This sounds reasonable enough until you realize that the seedling has to get through its first winter as a young plant before beefing up the following spring and exploding into flower. The bloom, emerging in late spring, lasts well into summer. As the colour drains from the oldest flowers at the base, buds at the tip of the spire break open. The blue goes well with the hairy, pale green lance foliage. In cooler gardens, the echium becomes a triennial, and has to negotiate two winters before flowering. Unless the second winter is particularly wet or cold, the echium will normally survive, as by this time it will have formed a woody trunk. It pays to protect it during the winter. At the Chelsea Physic Garden in London, groups of *E. pininana* grown next to a sunny wall have a rectangular frame, covered in fleece, placed over them. The frame keeps the fleece from pushing down on the stems.

Once the show is over, the plant shrivels and dies, leaving its woody hairy trunk as a forlorn reminder of its glorious past. Echiums self-seed easily in the ground around them. It is usually recommended that *E. pininana* is grown in full sun, yet at Mount Stewart in Northern Ireland various self-sown groups seem happiest when colonizing areas of partial shade.

Echiums have to be reserved for the most sheltered, driest and sunniest border you have. They are special plants and need cosseting. Most of us do not have those conditions, so we have to do our best to create them. A dry south- or west-facing wall is the ideal. Once it has flowered, died and self-seeded you can let it grow where it has fallen, even at the front of a bed, where it will look extraordinary and eyecatching. However, as it soars its basal leaves begin to wither on the stem, and instead of being well behaved and falling off they hang there, looking downright ugly until you pick them off. So ideally you need a plant with better foliage to be growing in front of it.

Echium blooms can reach 4m/13ft. This one is backed by flowering *Cordyline australis*, with sheltering pines in the background.

Echiums with their slender spires can be used in the same way as eremurus, the foxtail lily. Both have blooms that create height reminiscent of flowering agaves. A random effect works well with these plants. Their slender and gradually opening flowering stems lend themselves to being looked through. They enhance rather than obscure the view, so plant a few of them at the front of a border as satellites to a main group.

E. wildpretii, also from the Canaries, is only half hardy (0°C/32°F). Less tall, to about 2m/7ft, it has the same spire-like habit, only this time with red flowers. But the one to watch out for is the cross between the *E. wildpretii* and *E. pininana*: a hybrid which is, rightly, more spectacular than either of the above. Chiltern Seeds in Cumbria, who introduced them in 1991, remark that the base of the plant can be as thick as a man's leg and indeed it has to be strong to support the incredible 4m/14ft spire. The myriad flowers are Wedgwood blue. It has proved itself hardy in the UK.

Eremurus, its name deriving from the Greek *eremos*, meaning desert, and *oura*, meaning tail, is also known as the desert candle. This fleshy-rooted perennial, not bulb, is also referred to as a foxtail lily as the flowers resemble a fox's bushy tail. Eremurus can throw up a 3m/10ft column of white, pink or yellow, and as they flower in early and midsummer at the same time as echiums, you could indulge in a forest of different-coloured spires. The lance-shaped leaves tend to start dying off as the plant comes into flower. Once it has flowered an eremurus disappears, so you need to remember where it is – and have something up your sleeve to bridge the gap.

As eremurus do not take kindly to being overshadowed by other plants, keep the soil around them open. I lost mine beneath a fast-growing cistus. In their native habitat of the foothills of the Himalayas, the Middle East and Central Asia, they thrive in the open – mountainsides, grasslands or deserts; and it's important to remember that when planting. Although eremurus look tender, they are hardy perennials, to −5°C/23°F; like peonies they need winter cold to induce flowering. In their native habitat temperatures can fall to −40°C/0°F, but the plants survive because the plants are insulated below a thick blanket of snow. So in gardens in wetter, milder climates they are best mulched. Frost may catch the tender new growth in spring, so a dry mulch of gravel has a dual purpose. In a normal setting they should be self-supporting but because they are so slender and delicate-looking, plant them out of the teeth of the wind, or stake them.

An early-flowering white form, *Eremurus himalaicus*, grows to 2.5m/8ft. This is a good eremurus to start with, as it is more readily available than some, and in a sunny well-drained spot should be easy to establish without too much difficulty. *E. robustus* is another reliable one, with pale pink flowers in high summer on a stem rising to 3m/10ft. *E. stenophyllus* has dark yellow flowers to 1m/39in tall. Again it is easily obtainable, and its striking yellow flowers have ensured its popularity.

Unlike many frost-hardy plants, eremurus, which grows from a crown surrounded by fleshy roots, should be planted in the autumn. The soil must be well drained, so a layer of grit placed below when planting should ensure its survival. If you can feed it with potash at the same time, the results will be even more spectacular. It prefers alkaline soil, although it is not essential. Watch out for slug damage on the new emerging foliage.

Eremurus and eucomis can be confused, so it's important to clarify the difference. Eremurus are taller and more elegant, and the foliage dies off once the plants are in flower. More of a talking point for their uniqueness, eucomis are not as beautiful, but they are useful among other spiky plants: the flowers look as though they belong to them.

Hardy eucomis are bulbous perennials from South Africa, mostly native to high-altitude areas with summer rainfall, so in a more northerly climate they prefer ample moisture in a warm sunny spot. When summer is nearly over, the plant throws out a 15cm/6in spike of pale green flowers from the centre of its glossy leaves which are lance-shaped or strap-shaped. The similarly green flowering stem is flecked with purple blotches, rather like the leaves on the wild spotted orchid, *Dactylorhiza maculata*, but the flower is the thing. Above the purple-margined green flowers it has a funny little crown, just like the leaves erupting from the top of a pineapple – as suggested by the botanical name *Eucomis*, deriving from the Greek *eu* (good) and *kome* (tuft). It is easy to picture a plant whose common name is

Both *Echium wildpretii* **LEFT** and *Eremurus stenophyllus* **RIGHT** echo the shooting spire of *Agave filifera* (page 118).

pineapple flower, which refers to the crown of leafy bracts. Eucomis love plenty of sun – and if they can be planted at the base of a sunny wall, or tucked in by a rock which can offer extra heat and root protection, so much the better.

There are three species worth seeking out, which should be easily obtainable. The most dramatic is *Eucomis comosa*, reaching 75cm/30in or more. The flowers are pale green to cream, pink and purple. If you are a devotee of purple foliage, search out *E. 'Zeal Bronze'. E. bicolor* is easy to grow and has waxy jade-green flowers on a spire up to 60cm/24in. Look out also for greenish white *E. pallidiflora*, known as the giant pineapple flower, which can reach 1.75m/6ft in very warm climates, more likely 75cm/30in in cooler regions.

As the leaves are quite fleshy, eucomis make a good contrast with small grasses. Although they also require a well-drained position, they must not be allowed to dry out in summer – which could happen on light sandy or chalky soil. Again, it is useful to mulch in winter to protect against cold and wet, and, like eremurus, they do not like being crowded out, or over-shadowed by other plants.

Kniphofias, known as red-hot pokers, crackle from summer to autumn. The blaze of their reds, oranges and yellows is fitting in the heat of high summer, flaming right through to the dying embers of autumn. Their incandescent heads are thrust well above the lance-like leaves, which are forgettable in most species. One of the most imposing, in flower and foliage, with a finely toothed strappy leaf, is *Kniphofia caulescens*. The late-summer to autumn-flowering spikes (1.2m/4ft) are a seething coral-red, which bleaches out to pale yellow at the base. *K.* 'Prince Igor' burns a deep orange-red on a 1.8m/6ft spire in autumn. Amplify the effect by planting the smaller, later blooming and phosphorescent *K. rooperi* in front. Glowing orange-red from early to late autumn, and reaching up to 1.2m/4ft, it's a good, robust variety.

Kniphofias look best as a conflagration. You need at least a dozen or so plants to start a blaze, and if you have space for fifty or more you can almost warm your hands on them.

LEFT *Eremurus himalaicus* floating against the horizon at RHS Hyde Hall, Essex **ABOVE, TOP** Eucomis. **ABOVE, BOTTOM** *Kniphofia caulescens*.

STRAPS WITH GLOBE FLOWERS

The texture, shape and size of the architectural foliage described in the previous chapters are all key design issues. But the fun starts when you throw in a few jokers. Exhilarating contrasts emerge when you toss a few spheres among the vertical accents. Quite a few of the globe flowers described below have strappy leaves. Conveniently the strappy-leaved foliage echoes the architectural foliage.

The dandelion-clock blooms of allium bulbs are one of the most satisfying contrasts among verticals. Each flowerhead is like a thousand tiny stars held magically together in a perfect sphere. At first it looks as though the spherical flowers will contrast with the allium's own strappy foliage, but the leaves usually wither away as the buds break, the supporting naked stalks standing up like drinking straws.

The huge head of *Allium cristophii* is irresistibly tactile. Heads do not come much bigger than this one, which can have flowers reaching 19cm/7in on a 60cm/2ft stem. This larger flowering bulb makes a vivid contrast, crying out for bold leaves to keep it in perspective, especially as its own will have shrivelled away. In many ways the naked flower, minus the complication of foliage, allows you a simple contrast between it and whatever leaves you place with it.

Because alliums look as if they belong in dry, stony conditions – they come from dry mountainous areas mainly in the northern hemisphere – they look appropriate with arid-looking spiky evergreens such as yuccas. There is a practical growing consideration too: the lush foliage of plants such as cannas, phormiums and melianthus will shadow the ground, which is no good for alliums, which need full sun on the soil around them to perform well the following year, much in the way that tulip bulbs require a good baking.

All blossom is transient, so choose an allium that retains its seedheads. These last well into autumn, retaining the perfect sphere of the flowers, so you can keep the contrast going for longer. If you bring the dried heads inside the spheres will last indefinitely. The heads of *A. cristophii* are particularly durable. Look out for *A. giganteum* too. Its name referring to its stems, this giant may reach 1.5m/5ft, with 10cm/4in lilac-pink flowers.

Flowering later in the season, South African agapanthus has a similar effect. This perennial has strappy deep green leaves, a third of the length of the usually 60–90cm/24–36in flowering stalk. Not a leaf that is brimming with personality, but it does echo bolder straps. However, its chief glory is the flowers, a deep bluebell blue, which make rounded, pendent or intermediate umbels. Look out for deciduous-leaved species which come from moister mountainous grasslands and are hardier. Full sun and well-drained soil are essential for all agapanthus.

If you pot up agapanthus, the vigorous crowns become congested, and a juvenile plant will flower more quickly. The advantage is that you can bring out the pots to be enjoyed when the agapanthus is in full flower. Don't ignore repotting every couple of years or so, as the weight of root may burst open the pot. The plant may then take a year off while settling down once more. A good

TOP Bobbing spheres of *Allium aflatunense* contrasting with grasses in the background. **BOTTOM, LEFT TO RIGHT** *Allium karataviense* 'Ivory Queen'; *A.* 'Beau Regard'.

one for this treatment, as it is half hardy (0°C/32°F) and can be protected in winter, is *A. praecox* subsp. *orientalis,* which makes an evergreen clump and has flowering stems to 90cm/3ft. Those with evergreen leaves originate from coastal areas and are more tender.

Suitable for a garden with extrovert swords, fully hardy *A.* 'Blue Giant' lives up to its name with 15cm/6in rounded umbels of intense blue flowers. There are also fully hardy white ones such as *A.* 'Snowy Owl' which makes rounded umbels of white flowers late in the summer, also growing to the same height. Agapanthus flower from mid- to late summer. You can never go wrong extending colour into late summer.

STRAPS WITH LILY FLOWERS

Hemerocallis, or day lilies, have similar longer strappy leaves, but different-shaped trumpet flowers, which create contrast. There are so many varieties that you could have day lilies flowering from late spring to late summer. Their exotic flowers tie in with any exotic foliage around them.

Although the strappy leaves of hemerocallis tend to be scruffy, their first appearance in spring is most welcome. But their somewhat unkempt appearance by summer means that they incorporate best as part of a wild garden, or perhaps to bridge the gap between formal and wild areas, especially in light shade. In sharp gardening they are useful in a transition area between very spiky plants and a 'normal' area of garden. Their long flowering period, with each flower on a cluster of several, lasting just a day, is valuable, but once each flower has had its brief span, it hangs limply,

ABOVE Agapanthus Headbourne hybrids. **RIGHT** Delicate trumpets of *Hemerocallis lilioasphodelus* with *Nectaroscordum siculum* subsp. *bulgaricum* and thistly *Cirsium rivulare* in the background.

before dropping off. So at no time of flowering does the plant really look at its best; leaf and flower seem to be perpetually in some state of dishevelment. But we all know people like that and there is something engaging about their carefree appearance.

For the sharp garden you could seek out hemerocallis with spider-shaped or star-shaped flowers, rather than the rounder or triangular forms. The spidery ones seem to fit in best with the sharp, brittle look. *H.* 'Cat's Cradle' has spidery showy yellow flowers reaching about 90cm/3ft above narrow leaves. Consider also the earliest to flower, *H. dumortieri,* whose abundant yellow flowers are scented. The flowering stems reach 60cm/2ft high. Slightly taller at 66cm/26in is the more exotic-looking *H.* 'Anzac', which has large red lily-shaped flowers that flower in midsummer for several weeks.

Hemerocallis are fully hardy and can be pretty well left to their own devices. They prefer moist well-drained soil, but are pretty tolerant of drier conditions and will stand partial shade. In their native China, Korea or Japan, they are found in marshy river valleys, forest margins, mountainous areas and meadowland. They are vigorous, so fairly regular division ensures flowering. Congestion decreases their vitality.

Note that they are not totally drought-tolerant, so they need either a thick mulch or a slightly moist, free-draining area.

STRAPPY-LEAVED PLANTS TOLERANT OF SHADE

Frost-hardy *Iris confusa,* from China, is a strong evergreen flowering plant for shady spots. Reminiscent of bamboos, it has stems that fan out into quite broad leaves up to 40cm/16in long. It makes a clump about 1m/39in wide. It is best used for its evergreen foliage effect in awkward places, as the prolific springtime white flowers, splashed with purple or yellow spots, are short-lived.

Dianella tasmanica, from south-east Australia, including Tasmania, is also frost hardy and has cane-like stems. Its main appeal lies in its long-lasting dark blue berries. This is a rhizomatous perennial with stiff, strappy evergreen leaves reaching 1.2m/4ft tall, making a clump 45cm/18in wide. In early summer it produces small lavender-blue to violet flowers up to 2cm/¾in across. It likes a woodland area or a sheltered border in sun or partial shade, with soil from neutral to acid.

GROUND COVER

Ground cover is essential in any garden, so consider a couple of miniature plants that reflect the more dramatic leaves above them.

If you have a small area to fill, or want to make a miniature lawn with something other than grass, consider the foliage of sea thrift, *Armeria maritima,* a plant that offers strap-shaped leaves in miniature, roughly 4cm/1½in tall. This tough little sea thrift forms a dark green ground-covering cushion-like mat. From late spring onwards, for a month or so, it is covered in pink or purple drumstick flowerheads. It could be used as a ground cover around alliums to echo their larger globe flowers and colour.

Sea thrift also associates well with the strappy-leaved ophiopogon, also known as lilyturf, which sounds like a resting-place for fairies. Ophiopogons not only have similar leaves, but are in proportion as a planting companion. The dark green leaves of *Ophiopogon planiscapus* are only 10cm/4in long. A cushion of armerias with the broader and slightly taller ophiopogon leaves popping out of them would be a sharp garden in miniature. *O. planiscapus* 'Nigrescens' with its slightly arching purple-black foliage looks like a Lilliputian purple phormium. The tiny, somewhat dirty-looking white bell flowers are rather insignificant.

Frost-hardy *O. jaburan* 'Vittatus' makes a pleasing contrast with its marginal and striped creamy yellow bands on pale green leaves. This one reaches 60cm/2ft in height, with attractive short-stemmed white flowers. *O. japonicus* has dark green leaves 20cm/8in long. The flowers again are white, and bell-shaped. Because of their evergreen, uniform habit, ophiopogons make good edging plants, as well as ground cover.

DEVELOPING A DESIGN

When creating a garden design, develop a scheme or several schemes appropriate to your garden setting. In an open sunny location, you might favour a dry arid scene, with spiky plants appearing from cushions of rounded foliage, or a subtropical look, with the pointed paddle-shaped leaves of cannas and hedychiums.

Choose plants that are able to tolerate the same growing conditions. If you favour the arid look, combinations of agaves and yuccas look most appropriate with perennials that are equally hard-living and drought-tolerant. The choice you make will also depend on whether a plant looks right with its neighbours, unifying the planting scheme and creating a naturalistic effect. There is a very subtle dividing line as to whether a plant looks appropriate or not.

Not only do you have to think of the inspirational aspect – contrasts in shape and texture of foliage, and colour combinations; you also have to consider the practical issues regarding plant survival. Bear in mind that it is the suitability of the selected planting area that is most important. The location of a plant is crucial, for its survival depends on sun or shade, dry or moist soil, pH levels and fertility of the soil. With the majority of the plants in this chapter, there is no point in planting them in heavy shade. Faced with a garden with sunny and shady areas I reserve sun-loving plants for the sunny areas and shade-tolerant ones for the shady areas.

Crucial, too, is a plant's relationship to its neighbours – will it be swamped in a few years? – so you need to consider what to plant as a long-term specimen and what as a support plant, which may have to be removed after a few seasons, or tolerate being cut back hard and rejuvenated.

ABOVE Frosted blades of *Ophiopogon planiscapus* 'Nigrescens'.

COMBINATIONS

The most effective planting combinations rely on plants requiring the same conditions. Hostas may have foliage that looks good enough to eat in early summer, but they have no place next to an agave or yucca. Not only do they look unlikely bedfellows: they require different growing conditions.

For an arid-looking planting of spiky evergreens I would choose some of the following combinations. For early summer, alliums look good with yuccas – somehow the dry-looking flowerhead looks at home with the leaves of a yucca. The long-lasting dandelion-clock seedheads make their presence felt until you pick them or let them disintegrate. The startling yellows and oranges of kniphofias are similar to the flowers of aloes so you can make the garden look more exotic by growing these faux aloes. By all means grow aloes, but if you don't feel you have the right conditions, cheat with kniphofias. The coral-red flowers of *Kniphofia caulescens*, rising on stems up to 1.2m/4ft, are stunning, and the 1m/39in long leaves are suitably subtropical.

As well as shape, colours play an important part in focusing the mood of the finished garden. Blue flowers will cool down a subtropical mixture of spiky evergreens. Drifts of blue-spired *Echium candicans* have a soothing effect among the jagged sihouettes of palms and succulents. Blue flowers also complement the glaucous foliage of succulents such as agaves, aloes and yuccas. They contrast superbly with cream and golden variegated foliage. Or if you want to heat up an already heady brew of succulents, add flaming sulphur yellow eremurus or red hot kniphofias.

Alternatively, instead of choosing a hot or cold theme, you can let the whole garden explode with the full spectrum of colours available. If you wish to do this, reserve all the fiery yellows, oranges and reds for the sunnier areas of the garden. For areas with partial shade select those plants with cooler pastel colours. You can certainly get away with acanthus, echinops and teasels in a little shade. Then plant eryngiums, cardoon thistles and eucomis which are hungry for full sun, using them to contrast with the hot colours.

DESIGNING WITH THISTLE FLOWERS

Thistle flowers act as focal points among pointed leaves. The round heads of prickly echinops thistles, for instance, contrast with the vertical lines of lance shapes. Tall plants especially, which stand up and above plants at a lower level, act as flowering punctuation marks between large evergreen specimens. Thistle leaves are often prickly or finely cut, as in onopordums or *Cynara cardunculus*, which contrast with lance-like foliage surrounding them. Appearing as a mass of spines, the buds part and open up for the fluffy powder-puff flower inside. Although the long narrow leaves of the common teasle, *Dipsacus fullonum*, are featureless, they end in a point; but it is their prickly cone flowers, which remain unblemished throughout the winter, that are so useful, as they last so long.

Bold swords seem to demand barbed perennials to go with them. Spiny eryngiums pack a punch. They are spiny enough to look as though they have emerged from a spiky-leaved plant around them and as many of them grow to about 1m/39in tall they are good middle-storey plants in the border. The effect is more telling with large-scale plantings. It is futile to plant, say, one eryngium next to one yucca, even in a small garden; much better to plant three yuccas with at least nine eryngiums. The dagger-like leaves are enhanced by a cloud of steely blue flowers, which in high summer will be a metropolis for droning bees and insects.

This style of planting helps you to create a complete garden picture. Bulk up drifts of plants with self-seeders such as echinops and libertia, and biennials such as echium, onopordum and teasel (*Dipsacus fullonum*). Some plants have other methods for colonizing a new area. Acanthus, for instance, shoot up runners. The thing with these plants is to let them pop up in surprising places. Leave them and you may be inspired by combinations you had never anticipated.

Deciding whether the perennial you are choosing to fit in with spiky neighbours requires the same growing conditions – most of the ones discussed here have been selected because they do – is important. But there is more to it than that. Consider the whole look of a plant: its scale, its size and the colour of its flowers. I would not advocate putting a tall perennial such as *Cynara cardunculus* in the middle of an agave border. It would look too lush. Acanthus would associate better. Eryngiums look appropriate with yuccas – the hard spiny flowers, and matt leaves; echiums, with their matt leaves, covered in tiny hairs, also look right. *Silybum marianum* has glossy leaves – will that look right? Yes, indeed it will. It may sound confusing, but you can soon develop an eye for attractive combinations. Personal taste dictates the final choice.

Sky-stabbing *Cynara cardunculus* echoes the stark shapes of desert gardens.

DESIGNING WITH FLOATING SPIRES

Spires are useful in mass plantings or as dot plants. Incorporate them into your design to echo the natural flowering shapes of key specimens – from agaves to yuccas – that throw out spires of inflorescences. Very few of us gardening in a cool climate can hope for the massive stems and sky-piercing foxtail spires extending to over 4m/14ft seen on some succulents in hot countries, but you can copy the effect by planting perennials which contribute the same dramatic silhouettes.

Flowering spires help unify the garden, looking appropriate with drought-loving daggers. Like these plants they are set off to best advantage when planted against a bare sky or distant countryside. The theatrical effect is lost if they are surrounded by other plants and dense foliage.

Using a range of plants of differing sizes creates visual interest. If you can grow a 4m/13ft tall biennial such as *Echium pininana* you echo the gigantic spiky inflorescences of agaves, furcraeas and yuccas, creating a vision of larger-than-life plants luxuriating in warmer climates than our own. Eremurus, coming in a different range of heights, can create interest on several levels. Acanthus are excellent as middle-height plants. Eucomis, which have flowers on shorter stems, bed in happily with other bromeliad plants such as puyas and fascicularias.

Contemporary gardening has demonstrated that planting schemes need not require a strict gradation of plants in height from the lowest at the front to the tallest at the back of the border – the horticultural equivalent of the school photograph. The traditional approach, with lavender or cranesbills in the foreground and ram-rod straight delphininiums staked to within an inch of their lives at the back, often looks too regimented. It's time to accept a more informal and random approach. Plants can be placed in the foreground deliberately or allowed to self-seed. It helps a design to make the planting look more casual, and less contrived. After all, how many plants in the wild naturally place themselves with the tallest at the back? They don't. Certain plants can be allowed to appear as if they have broken off from the main family group, seeming to have colonized a new area – which is a natural form of survival in the wild. If a self-seeded plant arrives on the edge of the border and you have the urge to tidy it up, don't. Leave it, even if the chosen resting place seems wayward. Once you start fiddling unnecessarily it may look contrived. However, if it lands in completely the wrong place you may have to tweak a little. You are allowed to cheat by planting it to make it look as though it has decided to land at the front of the border accidentally. Keep your garden landscape from becoming too predictable. Some of the plants described in this chapter could be planted as wild cards, to add interest in unexpected places, perhaps as a large plant cropping up near the front of a bed, and to prevent the garden looking too orderly and more natural. Make it look as though nature has a hand in it, not just you, the omnipotent gardener. Planting this way is fun, too. Making a garden look as though the planting has happened by accident can produce pleasant surprises. Who knows what pleasure you will derive from an unexpected partnership of plants? Next year you build on it further. Nothing has to be permanent.

Good designs are often enhanced by throwing a few rogues into the pot. A skeletal backbone,

Toothed foliage and blazing aloe spikes at the Kotoske Garden, Phoenix, Arizona. You can copy these with kniphofias in temperate gardens.

fleshed out with perennials, is likely to be a well-behaved static arrangement. Apart from the natural spread of the plants, the design will not change much. To add variety and interest, you can either cheat by shoehorning some plants into odd or unexpected places in your initial design, or plant various self-seeders, which will ingratiate themselves within your planting. If you decide to cheat, plant some tall eremurus to provide verticals near the front of the border. They will look as though they have self-seeded. Likewise you could do this with bulbs such as alliums or clump-forming perennials such as agapanthus. Create depth by choosing a plant that lends itself to being peered through, especially those with attractive seedheads, that provide even longer interest. However, be wary of allowing teasels, *Dipsacus fullonum*, to run riot. I did so once and came to regret it. You soon have forests of them. Sometimes

you have to be hard and hoe out the excess ones, or offer them to the unwary.

This style of planting creates perspective, as a tall plant at the front breaks all the rules about height and automatically seems to make a border seem deeper, and looks more naturalistic. It's also refreshing to have the opportunity to see flowers close to, especially on a perennial normally relegated to the back. And if you choose a plant that can be looked through, so much the better, as this is an even more effective way of playing around with perspective. Although not sharp, the short-lived perennial *Verbena bonariensis* is now an object lesson for this style of planting. Its airy branches and generous clusters of small flowers lend themselves to being looked through. Once it self-seeds, its progeny can be left in situ to create delightful effects wherever it lands in the border. It is used like this in the exotic garden at Great Dixter. Less airy plants, such as *Cynara cardunculus*, when placed in the foreground, perform the same function. To avoid this style of planting looking eccentric, you have to back up the self-seeders, or clumps you have placed, with a cluster of what look like parent plants as a main group. And the more often you discipline yourself with repeated plantings of particular species, the more unified the design will be.

DESIGNING WITH GLOBE FLOWERS WITH STRAPPY LEAVES

Although globe-flowered plants with strappy leaves have foliage that echoes the larger strap-shaped foliage of key plants, it is the globes themselves, adding contrast to angular shapes around them, that make the greatest impact within a design. At its simplest, in including them

LEFT Prickly towers of cacti in Arizona offer shapes that the sharp gardener can borrow. **ABOVE** A simple container of aloes, contrasting with the horizontal planes of the table and wall.

you make the same contrasts as in a game of noughts and crosses. The circles and random crosses create a pleasing picture in their own right. You just have to decide whether you want more of one than the other.

Agapanthus, with their big blue globe flowers, are must-have perennials. The gardener who wants to squeeze out a number of seasonal combinations would do well to plant drifts of alliums among or behind clumps of agapanthus. Retaining their foliage while flowering, agapanthus work well with alliums, whose foliage dies down to nothing. And the foliage never gets in the way of spiky evergreen foliage. The globe flowers on most alliums appear from late spring to early summer, so use them to fill the early summer gap before agapanthus take over.

It is better to plant earlier-flowering plants towards the back so that later-flowering plants are up front for their moment of glory. The combination of the alliums' ghostly globe seedheads echoing the agapanthus is like a bobbing sea of spheres. Alliums also go well with the glossy lushness of phormiums. It makes sense to pair blues, purple and violets with cream or golden variegated foliage to show them to best advantage. Plant them with *Yucca gloriosa* 'Variegata' or *Phormium* 'Yellow Wave'.

DESIGNING WITH PERENNIALS

Finally, when I create a design I am interested in perennials that have a long flowering season. If they don't, they have to compensate for a brief flowering period by dying beautifully. Seedpods or good seedheads can be more heart-stopping than flowers. I have never been a devotee of the spring flush either. There is so much to enjoy in other peoples' gardens in spring, after all – why gild the lily? Once the first flush of spring-flowering bulbs is over, and after most blossoming shrubs have delighted us for long enough, peaking by midsummer, perennials have to take over. Spring bulbs are too transient and shrubs take up too much room. Few gardens have the space for those spring- and early-summer-flowering ones – forsythia, lilac, philadelphus or weigela, and for many gardeners, if you plant in this vein, it is inevitably much harder to keep up the show from midsummer onwards. It seems logical to plant for climaxes in mid- to late summer, especially as this is when the days are supposed to be warmest, the time of the year for sitting out.

ABOVE A spiky bouquet of *Eryngium agavifolium* and agapanthus blooms.

The RHS garden at Hyde Hall in Essex is on a most unpromising site for sharp gardening. The surrounding wheat fields leave the area exposed to dry south-westerly winds in summer and freezing Siberian gales in winter. The climate is more one of extremes than that of the milder west-coast UK. Although the low annual rainfall of only 60cm/2ft is in the garden's favour, and the south-facing site maximizes all the sunshine there is, the clay soil is heavy and unstable, which means that it is not free-draining. The earth can set like concrete in dry periods and is so claggy as to be unworkable in the wet winter months. Yet in spite of all these factors that appear to knock the idea of successful dry gardening on the head, the creation of a dry garden here has been most successful.

As drainage is the key factor in the survival of plants used in sharp gardening and clay is one of the main bars to their successful cultivation, the soil is carefully prepared before planting, as described to me by former curator Matthew Wilson. The staff excavate the soil to a depth of 60cm/2ft, forking over the hard 'pan' underneath. As it is all too easy to create a 'sumping effect', they add 1cm/½in perforated drainage pipe, taking into account the fall of the land. This pipe is then covered with 1.2cm/1in of drainage stone, to disperse the water.

They then replace the soil to a depth of 20cm/8in, adding a 1cm/½in layer of 6mm sandy grit, forking in each layer and gently firming it. They repeat this until the right level is reached and leave it for at least a week for the soil to settle before planting. After planting, they wait for a couple of weeks, so that any rain goes straight into the ground, before adding a gravel mulch. This mulch – a mixture of 20mm and 30mm stone that has to be spread carefully to avoid damaging the base of the plants – suppresses weeds and allows moisture to be retained throughout the growing season. A geotextile layer underneath is not required, as the 7cm/3in mulch is considered deep enough to keep weeds out, and allows ornamental perennials and annuals to self-seed. In addition, great use has been made of bulbs which grow happily through mulch but not through sheeting.

Survival of the plants has not been left to chance. All the plants chosen have been selected for their tenacity in withstanding long periods of drought during an East Anglian summer. They are from arid climates, most supporting themselves with long root systems, which seek out moisture and guard against wind rock in an open location such as this. The bright light under the open East Anglian sky can make pastel shades appear bland, but hot spicy colours stand up well in these conditions.

As seasonal weather patterns become less reliable, and with increasing demands on water resources, the ability to cultivate plants without the need for artificial irrigation becomes all the more important. Hyde Hall demonstrates its commitment to preserving water with this style of gardening, which can be modified for the smaller private garden.

An exploration of Hyde Hall's dry garden reveals its emphasis on flowering plants in a large site. Illustrating the fact that most

successful gardens work best with some kind of evergreen backbone, there is a good sprinkling of architectural plants such as yuccas – *Y. filamentosa, Y. flaccida* 'Ivory', *Y. gloriosa* and *Y. whipplei* – phormiums, varieties of pines including *Pinus mugo* and *P. sylvestris* cultivars, the European dwarf fan palm *Chamaerops humilis*, *Fascicularia bicolor* and junipers. These spiky shapes are highlighted with the softer shapes of fast-growing, hard-living Mediterranean plants such as broom, cistus, euphorbia, hebe, lavender and rosemary. This style of contrasting planting immediately creates a conflict of shapes that is ripe for an overlay of the kinds of appropriate flowering plants described in this chapter.

At Hyde Hall these include the globe flowers of alliums and agapanthus, adding further contrast. At home with a wide variety of different textures, the alliums fit in with the dry look of yuccas. Spires such as *Acanthus spinosus, Eremurus himalaicus, E. stenophyllus,* and *Kniphofia caulescens* all create height. Thistle flowers of *Echinops bannaticus* 'Taplow Blue', *E. ritro* and several eryngiums planted in drifts make hazy blue clouds of spiky blossom through which the spiky evergreens burst.

LEFT Swords of phormium and slinky spires of *Verbascum bombyciferum* are more telling when planted against a flat horizon, as at the RHS garden at Hyde Hall in June. Note the boulders, bobbing alliums in the distance and the shrubby mound of the curry plant, *Helichrysum italicum* subsp. *serotinum* (left), making good foils. **RIGHT, TOP** The spiral inflorescence and bayonet leaves of *Yucca gloriosa*. **RIGHT, BOTTOM** *Eryngium pandanifolium*.

Using perennials among spiky foliage plants

In Santa Monica, California, garden designer Mary Effron is bowled over by spiky foliage plants with architectural shapes and textures. She tailors her initial design decisions to her clients' tastes and the architecture of their home, but believes that a garden consisting only of soft, finely textured plants such as lavender and rosemary, jasmine and penstemon cries out for bold contrasting plants such as agaves, phormiums or yuccas. To her mind, these plants make the garden come alive, helping to create a cohesive design in which the architectural spiky plants are balanced with the fluffy plants.

Although playing around with these shapes is striking, once she starts working with colour combinations, the effect is even more exciting. Simply placing a red phormium with the grey-green of an artemisia is a pleasing combination. The red- or bronze-leaved phormiums also go brilliantly with chocolate pelargoniums. Mary likes to combine blues with each other, such as *Agave attenuata* with the blue grass *Festuca glauca* and *Echeveria secunda*. Glaucous-leaved *Agave americana* with blue or deep purple-blue flowering spires of *Echium fastuosum* works well.

One of Mary's favourite planting schemes contrasts the same agave with *Lavandula* x *allardii*. She also finds that strong flowering shrubs such as *Leonitis leonurus*, which has an orange-red flowering stem growing to 2m/7ft with lance-shaped foliage, make a good backdrop to any spiky plant.

Once the key plants have been selected, Mary adds perennials and ground-cover plants such as verbena, oregano and thyme to connect the planting and smooth out the rough edges of what could easily turn into a severe landscape. They also add necessary seasonal colour.

One of Mary's golden rules, space permitting, is to plant the chosen spiky plants in threes or fives to create the maximum dramatic impact and for a more telling effect. Mary enjoys placing spiky plants such as variegated phormiums in individual large, rustic containers, surrounded by echiums.

Mary's recipe for soil preparation is simple. She uses 60 per cent garden soil, 15 per cent organic compost (a few products are added together to create a balanced medium), 25 per cent pumice for drainage and some granulated all-purpose fertilizer such as 12–12–12, applied as per the instructions on the bag. In southern California, the heavy clay soil has to be lightened with gypsum, which loosens up the soil, but if you do this remember that it will preclude growing lime-hating plants.

At Mary Effron's garden in Santa Monica a snout of *Agave attenuata* emerges from lavender with potted phormiums and *Echium candicans* in the background.

Lavish planting on a grand scale overlooking Morecambe Bay

Most of us plan our gardens for outdoor leisure and colour through the summer. But when high summer is past, what then? If we plan for masses of colour for the transient summer months, for every summer flowering plant nurtured, unless space is unlimited, we must often dispense with another plant that would have given us winter interest.

Jonathan Denby's garden and woodland at Yewbarrow House in Grange-over-Sands, with sweeping views of Morecambe Bay, extends to 1.8 hectares/4½ acres, so he has the space to plan a garden for all seasons. Further, Jonathan

strongly believes that a garden's design should anticipate the need for vistas seen from within the house. Many gardens may be enjoyed only if you are actually within them, which is unfortunate if the weather is unkind or if you are standing at the kitchen sink or seated at your desk. Jonathan and his wife Margaret are a busy couple: with three daughters under ten, and running their own business, their hands are full. Gardening is pursued on the run. As their close neighbour and an exotic plants enthusiast, I was asked to work with Jonathan in the creation of a subtropical garden. We think,

Cordylines, *Phormium tenax* and *Trachycarpus fortunei* punctuate the garden at Yewbarrow House in Cumbria.

given our 'Cumbrian Riviera' setting, that we can grow many of the plants that until a few years ago were considered safe only in Cornish gardens.

The garden is now divided into various themed areas, the majority designed to be enjoyed from within the house. He has a sunken garden that can be viewed from his study, a temple garden seen from the kitchen, and a Japanese garden seen from the master bedroom. So much is on view because the garden enjoys a sloping site, dished towards the house like an amphitheatre, allowing him to look up from the house and see most of the garden reaching up behind to the rising ground beyond.

If one of your design priorities is to enjoy the greater part of the garden from behind glass, you need something to refresh your eye when you are most often indoors – through the winter months. A sunken garden is as fresh and green in January as it is in August. What used to be an uninteresting limestone chipping parking area in front of the house is now an exotic arena displaying hardy palms and exotic evergreens. Its focal point is a cabbage palm, *Cordyline australis*, imported from a specialist nursery as a mature specimen and used to create impact and to impart an air of maturity. The cars are now relegated to the far end of this part of the garden, screened by a specially created casually tumbledown stone wall. Some existing planting had to be relocated. When he began working on the garden there were about ninety hydrangeas, most of them in this prominent area, all of which have now been found homes elsewhere, for the

simple reason that the fleeting seasonal pleasure they give is ruined by the need to look at their skeletons for the next six months.

My own fondness for exotic evergreens seems to be infectious and I admit to influencing Jonathan in this respect. Jonathan's brief for the design included the admonition, 'And remember, I don't want too many spiky plants!' He now shares with me an absorbing passion for anything remotely sharp-looking. He is hooked. This style of gardening is particularly well suited to Grange's kind climate. Some say Grange enjoys the best microclimate in Cumbria, with its south-east-facing location overlooking Morecambe Bay. On moving to Yewbarrow House, Jonathan wanted to capitalize on the favourable climate, and has sought to establish in his garden as many tender and unusual subtropical plants as possible. Recalling visits to subtropical Cornish gardens, he has indulged his passion for bright red flowers, with a selection of brilliant scarlet rhododendrons, and later, from high summer, fiery cannas blaze well into autumn. In the early planning stages I cautioned Jonathan about a familiar problem: far too many gardens peak by the end of June. So the design brief included planting with the whole of the year in mind. The garden is particularly fine in late summer, with masses of agapanthus popping out among yuccas and phormiums.

For what is still very much a new garden, only in its fourth season, there is a great deal to enjoy. Last winter Jonathan created a new planting area hard against the boundary wall beyond the walled garden, bringing back into cultivation what had become a wilderness and using a large expanse of unheated polytunnel (the plastic well out of sight behind the walled garden), so that Jonathan's increasing collection of tender subtropical bedding is now protected in the winter. He continues to reduce the lawn areas to make way for more borders and plants. I always advise caution, but am usually overruled!

Jonathan's pet project is to illuminate the garden to draw the maximum enjoyment from it during the winter evenings. This is why architectural evergreens are so vital to the design: their silhouettes lend themselves to being well lit.

Repetition of spiky outlines and perennials unify a large border. In a south-facing well-drained border over porous limestone at Yewbarrow, blue and white agapanthus, scarlet crocosmia and eryngiums (foreground) complement the flowering yucca to the left and cordylines on the right. Daisy-flowered South Africa *Osteospermum jucundum* make a mat along the front of the border. Note how the crocosmia and agapanthus leaves echo the spiky foliage.

Fluffy
spikes

PREVIOUS PAGES *Pennisetum orientale.*
RIGHT Annual grasses: *Briza maxima*
takes centre stage in a group of
terracotta pots at Wave Hill, New York
City, with *Lamarckia aurea* to the front.

Fluffy spikes

Floating, feathery grasses to add the finishing touch

Grasses possess crisp outlines, whispering foliage and offer a great variety of textures. I count them as sharp because the tips of the leaves end in points, but it is their featheriness that makes them so desirable in sharp gardening: when contrasted with spikes, frothing grasses accentuate the rigid outlines of sharp foliage plants. And just as gardens benefit from the evergreen qualities of many sword-like plants, the autumn and winter advantages of grasses enrich a design for those months when foliage and seedheads have to be relied upon to sustain interest.

GRASSES INSTEAD OF LAWN

Sharp gardening involves changing the emphasis of preconceived notions of garden style. Think again about the ubiquitous lawn surrounded by narrow flower borders. Grass as lawn in the centre of the garden is rather like an inverted picture frame. Instead of all the interest occupying the middle of the frame, the focus of the garden (flowers) is banished to the perimeters (borders) and, eccentrically, pride of place is given to the central void. This is all rather odd from a design point of view.

Grass has been endemic to gardens and gardening for centuries. The Tudors found grass useful for playing bowls on, but grass as lawn did not take off until landowners in the seventeenth century began to develop large gardens. Lawns became a status symbol, as they have to be maintained, either by grazing animals or by men with scythes. By the nineteenth century, when mechanical lawnmowers were invented, having a garden without a lawn was unthinkable for the middle classes in Europe and North America.

But today lawns no longer seem so essential. As space for people and gardens becomes tighter, a manicured green rug seems a greedy way of gardening. With threatened water shortages, even in the UK during the odd hot, dry summer, and the effects of global warming, it's good to question whether all the watering and maintenance necessary for a lawn is environmentally friendly. A square metre/yard of well-tended turf takes more feeding, spraying and fussing over than any

other like-sized area of the garden. It is hard to remain ecologically sound when firing up a petrol or electric lawnmower and showering the lawn with chemical weed or moss killers and fertilizers. Moreover, for most people lawns spell hours of unremitting summer toil, but the revolution in our lifestyle means that finding the time to tend the grass is becoming increasingly difficult. These days, busy mums are often at work rather than at home, so less able to snatch the odd few minutes in the garden, and the Sunday ritual of dads mowing the lawn is a thing of the past. In spite of more gadgets being on offer to save time, people have never had less time at their disposal.

Nonetheless, for many people lawns serve a useful purpose, especially as they often take up more than three quarters of the garden. To have the garden filled for the most part with a known quantity such as a lawn can be a relief for a novice gardener surveying their new plot anxiously. It is like being faced with an essay to write and finding most of the page already completed. However, when houses and gardens were created on a larger scale, you needed the space dedicated to a lawn to set off the house and garden, but now that gardens are getting smaller, there isn't quite that same anxiety to fill the space and there are countless other materials available with which to floor your garden.

A lawn does not readily lend itself to a design that embodies a contemporary planting of spiky plants. Hard-textured plants usually look more appropriate among pebbles, gravel or shards of slate. So if you are tired of lawn, and recognize that a rectangle of green stripes is not the best way of presenting your take on sharp gardening, why not abandon it?

But grass has another purpose to serve: it can not only set off plants and home but also become a resting place for the eye. It's an antidote to the busyness of borders. If you seek the change of tempo that grass creates, while lacking the space for lawn, the trend for adding grasses to border plantings is heaven-sent. Instead of laying down a lawn like so many strips of carpet, you can incorporate tufts of grasses among showier flowering plants. Grasses immediately offer a different texture with their leaf blades and a lightness of touch as they weave themselves through other foliage, creating unexpected patterns. And with grasses there is always constant movement: many blow and sway in the lightest of breezes. The movement is an excellent foil to the rigid spear-like leaves of succulents. The combination of spikes and fluffiness excites and alerts the eye to the endless possibilities of foliage, which can be enjoyed without relying on brightly coloured flowers.

Grasses' soft outlines float between spiky subjects. As contrast they also look good with the rounded shapes of Mediterranean and Australasian plants such as cistus, euphorbias, pittosporums and hebes. If you have a windy spot, there can be few better choices than grasses, especially as the flickering foliage adds an elegance not many other plants can match. Remember too that the vertical lines of grasses lend themselves to being reflected in water, especially if they have pale green or variegated foliage, as brighter colours always pick up the light better.

Associating well with perennials, they also come into their own when used as a contrast with arid-looking spiky plants such as agaves and yuccas and globe-like bulbs such as alliums. They require the same well-drained, sunny conditions, and look so appropriate with them that it is curious that they have not been planted together more.

TOP Gossamer-like *Stipa gigantea* threads through *Allium* 'Globemaster'. **BOTTOM** A cloud of *Verbena bonariensis* and *Calamagrostis* x *acutiflora* 'Karl Foerster' in the late September sun at RHS Hyde Hall.

As they age so gracefully in late autumn and winter, grasses are able to pull their weight in gardening's darkest season. By that time shrubs are a spent force and many perennials have been cut down, apart from the few whose wintry skeletons still sustain architectural interest, and gardens are looking bleak. Grasses and evergreen spiky plants come to the rescue. In addition, if the winter is seasonally cold, grasses take on a magical quality in frost and provide a platform for a light dusting of snow. Winter is when grasses come into their own: they often look at their best in freezing conditions, especially in brilliant winter sunlight.

What is the attraction of grasses? With infinite varieties of colours ranging from greens to golds and creams, plus rich textures both in the flowers and leaves, their appeal is enormous.

Foliage colour
- Foliage is predominantly green, but highlighted either with margins, stripes or splashed with paler colours.
- Gold and red foliage is particularly coveted.
- In autumn, when colour is draining from other perennials, grasses offer an inspirational blast of colour that lasts through autumn into winter.

Forms
- Grasses may be tall, thrusting, upright and columnar, or fan out.
- Some form cushioned mounds of dense foliage.
- There are also tufty grasses with short bristly leaves.
- Others form graceful fountains of foliage.

Flowers
- The flowers of grasses have a much longer life than most perennials.
- Plumes of flowers illuminated by the sun look like fiery torches.
- Some spikelets of flowers are flattened, some are more rounded.

Textures
- Foliage can be curly, flat or pleated.
- Leaves may be bent, rolled over or straight-edged.
- The tactile qualities of grasses are apparent in the foliage, which can be matt or glossy, and the flowerheads can be silky or fluffy.
- Some flowers look like heads of wheat, some like rabbits' tails, some like peacock feathers.

Thirty years on from the days when pampas grass was the nation's top grass, a greater variety of grasses is now available. These are highly prized and collectible, and the number to covet grows

CLOCKWISE FROM TOP LEFT *Miscanthus sinensis* 'Strictus'; *Pennisetum macrourum*; *Agave striata* var. *falcata* looking grass-like; *Elytrigia elongata* 'José Select'.

larger every year. But it took a long time for gardeners to see the light with grasses. For many years they were ignored, or planted without a clear idea of how to show them off to their best advantage. They have never enjoyed the limelight until now, perhaps because they are not as showy as flowering shrubs or perennials. Because there wasn't the market, they weren't readily available. It was not until the 1950s that grasses gradually became more popular, when Karl Foerster saw their potential for maintaining interest in the freezing winters of Germany and continental Europe.

Nowadays, you could say that the lawn is moving over to the borders. The leading exponents for creating dramatic effects with grasses are Piet Oudolf in the Netherlands, Rosemary Weisse in Munich, and Wolfgang Oehme and James van Sweden in the United States. Oudolf follows the European trend for planting grasses and perennials as pioneered by Foerster, while the Americans take their inspiration from the great prairies, and plant in generous concentrated blocks.

All grasses have narrowly linear leaves, ending in a point; they are fined-down versions of swords and lances. Bear in mind the following points before choosing any:

- Grasses are versatile, associating well with other plants in a border or a container.
- They often look at their best from late summer to early winter.
- Many provide continued interest from late winter to early spring.
- A good way of making grasses look natural is to plant several of one species.

Here are some of the most useful perennial grasses before I explore the contrasts of grasses with the rigid forms of spiky evergreens.

GRASSES AND SEDGES FOR DAMP AREAS

Carex (sedges) prefer moist soils that do not get waterlogged. They like sun or partial shade and are happy in average garden soil as long as it does not dry out. Most carex are fully hardy apart from the New Zealand ones such as *C. conica, C. morrowii* and their cultivars, which are not reliably hardy when temperatures fall below −7°C/19°F.

The gold ones are highly attractive. *C. siderosticha* 'Variegata' has deciduous broad leaves 2cm/1in wide, which is wide for a grass, and 25cm/10in long, having a spread of 40cm/16in in due course. It is fully hardy and makes a low clump of pale green leaves, margined and striped white, with beigey-brown flower spikes in late spring. The leaves can be used to echo bolder plants such as cream and green variegated yucca, in particular *Y. gloriosa* 'Variegata'.

Carex elata 'Aurea' is one of the finest hardy deciduous golden sedges. The leaves, extending to 60cm/2ft long, are predominantly gold with thin green margins. The flowering stems reach 50cm/20in, with brown male flower spikes. The plant clumps up to 70cm/28in tall and 45cm/18in wide.

Also fully hardy, *Hakonechloa macra* 'Aureola' has become popular in recent years because of its brilliant yellow or golden arching leaves up to 25cm/10in. A slender green stripe shoots down the centre of the leaf, which turns pinky-red in autumn. It makes a vibrant show, although it has zero interest in winter, when the deciduous foliage is best cut down. But from summer to late autumn it is gorgeous. Its light green needle-like spikelets appear late in the season, roughly 18cm/7in long.

It can cope with partial shade, but does best in moist well-drained soil in full sun. Its dynamic leaf also makes it a worthy contender as a container-grown specimen.

Another grass for moist areas is the fully hardy evergreen *Deschampsia cespitosa* (tussock grass). Its feathery silver plumes, from early to late summer, reach 2m/7ft high, spreading to 1.5m/5ft wide. *D. flexuosa* is also evergreen (and hardy), with foliage growing to 20cm/8in long. Its common name, wavy hair grass, perfectly describes its wavy silver purple or brown spikelets. *D. flexuosa* prefers acid soil but *D. cespitosa* will happily cope with neutral. Don't let either of them dry out. In damper climates, as in the UK, *D. cespitosa* may suffer from rust.

TALLER GRASSES FOR DAMP BUT WELL-DRAINED SOIL

If you wish to grow taller grasses, consider miscanthus. These self-supporting plants work well as large specimens at the back of a border or as a windbreak. Preferring moist meadows in the wild, they enjoy sunny, well-drained but moist conditions in gardens. Frost-hardy silver banner grass, *Miscanthus sacchariflorus*, is a sturdy form – almost subtropical, as its stems are reminiscent of bamboo canes. It is deciduous, but the leaves turn to a rich straw colour, and stand up well in strong winds. Looking good until the spring, this is a grass you can bank on for nine months of the year. The blue-green leaves around 90cm/3ft long have light green midribs, and the stems will reach 2.5m/8ft.

There is a rash of cultivars associated with hardy *M. sinensis*, also known as Japanese silver grass. *M. sinensis* is similar to *M. sacchariflorus*, liking the same conditions, but the whole plant dies off by midwinter, so it needs cutting down in spring. Look out for *M.s.* 'Silberfeder' (Silver Feather), grown for its pink-brown panicles that show well from early autumn. It normally reaches 2.5m/8ft. Because the zebra grass, *M.s.* 'Zebrinus', is more arching, the overall habit is more open. Its pale yellow-white leaves give it a dappled, camouflage effect.

Tussock-forming frost-hardy *Chionochloa conspicua* is a tufted evergreen grass. The 1.2m/4ft mid-green leaves have a hint

TOP TO BOTTOM *Hakonechloa macra* 'Aureola'; *Deschampsia cespitosa* 'Goldgehänge'; *Miscanthus sinensis* 'Variegatus', *Allium hollandicum* 'Purple Sensation' and *Geranium* 'Bressingham Flair'.

of red-brown on them. These narrow leaves are similar to those of their relatives, the cortaderias. The creamy white flowers are delicate and fragile-looking, but the stems are strong and arching. They will reach 2m/7ft, and bulk up to 1m/39in. The smaller tussock grass *C. rubra* is evergreen with narrow ochre-red leaves, which turn shades of warm pink and red in winter. It reaches 75cm/30in high with a spread of 30cm/12in. Chionochloas don't appreciate winter wet and must have good drainage.

GRASSES SUITABLE FOR HOT, DRY AREAS

Until the early 1990s the market in grasses was cornered by the hardy pampas grass, *Cortaderia selloana*. Its tall rigid plumes graced many a front garden from the 1970s onwards. Familiarity, though, should not breed contempt. One should not be too hard on pampas: in the right place, and given enough space, it can be a highly prized plant. However, to show off its plumes it is best planted at the rear of a border with a dark green backdrop. Sadly it is too large for most gardens, soon dwarfing its neighbours, as many gardeners have found to their cost. You may wish to remove it. It is a tenacious plant to get rid of or cut back and the leaves are guillotine-sharp, so wear gloves when handling it. If it is in a safe enough spot (not close to your neighbours' x *Cupressus leylandii* hedge which you are dying to get rid of), torching it certainly stops it in its tracks. When I decided to remove my own ten-year-old specimen (planted unwittingly by myself), I burned as much as possible first, but it was still the devil's own job to dig the root out. To ensure no possible

ABOVE Spiky blades and feathery plumes to add contrast in sharp designs: *Miscanthus sinensis, Calamagrostis* x *acutiflora* 'Strictus', *Miscanthus* 'Hermann Mussel' and *Stipa calamagrostis* in mid-August at RHS Wisley.

reappearance of the wretched thing I filled the void by sinking a water tank to make a small pond there. I can confidently say there has not been a flicker of pampas grass since. The 3m/10ft flowering stems of *C. selloana* always seem to blow over at the first opportunity, leaving you to prune them out without cutting yourself. Their lopsidedness can make a garden look abandoned. Remember that *C. selloana*, with leaves reaching 1.2m/4ft, and bulking up to 2m/7ft, needs plenty of room, so allow for that, planting it in a position with plenty of sun and well-drained soil. Note that in California cortaderias are invasive, so plant with caution, if you plant at all.

Some of the cortaderias with variegated leaves make inspired focal points. The green foliage is worth brightening up, so choose a variegated form, which is less prolific in spread and flowering, but ultimately more satisfying than plain green. *C.s.* 'Aureolinata' (syn. 'Gold Band') has leaves that are predominantly gold-margined, with a narrow central green stripe, and about 2m/7ft long.

Frost-hardy *C. richardii* is much less poker-like. This New Zealand toe-toe grass has elegant, arching stems bearing silvery white panicles. The 2.5m/9ft stems that support them are so tough that they will last all winter, with the panicles becoming ever more ghostly. The rigid stems never seem to blow down at all, and can be left on if desired. The new stems emerge in midsummer and obscure the old ones. It is suitable for a wild area, perhaps difficult to negotiate, or where you don't go every day, because it can be left indefinitely, without looking scruffy; this grass looks after itself. The sabre-sharp leaves, to 1.2m/4ft, discourage munching predators.

ABOVE FROM LEFT Cortaderias need careful placing but can be breathtaking: *Cortaderia rendatleri* 'Rosea'; although fragile-looking, *Stipa gigantea* is surprisingly wind-tolerant.

Stipas are variously known as feather grass, needle grass and spear grass – all names indicative of their tactile and bristly qualities. There are over 300 species of these perennial deciduous or evergreen grasses. Most require full sun and well-drained soil.

If you want to run your hand through the stems, one of the best tactile grasses is hardy *Stipa tenuissima* or pony tails, which is feathery with greenish white and then buff panicles. The golden-green leaves are 30cm/12in long. This plant is so irresistible to the touch that it demands a spot where it can be easily appreciated – a raised bed by a path, say. By late summer it's like a shock of tousled blonde hair, each filament dancing in the slightest breath of wind. It remains beguiling throughout winter, especially when frosted – an unforgettable vision. Plant it where it will catch dramatic early morning or late afternoon sunshine and have your camera ready.

The evergreen pheasant's tail grass, *Anemanthele lessoniana* (syn. *Stipa arundinacea*), has fine winter colour. It keeps its summery orange-brown streaks in the same rich colour all winter. More versatile than most, it grows happily on heavier soils than many grasses and even stands partial shade. It is frost hardy. With an open, loose habit it has 30cm/12in leaves that arch gracefully, and in summer purple-green spikelets foam out of it. These qualities, and the fact that it looks good for most of the year, make it an excellent edging plant. It self-seeds, but not too alarmingly.

The open habit of the golden oats grass, *Stipa gigantea*, creates two effects. Grow it against a dark background to appreciate its golden oat-like panicles, or at the front of the border to create perspective and offer a transparent screen to look through and beyond. The anonymous semi-evergreen leaves grow quite densely, to about 70cm/28in long and are crowned with 2.5m/8ft stems bearing plumes of golden oats. In spite of its fragile-looking drinking-straw stems, *S. gigantea* holds up well; heavy rain more than wind is responsible for weighing the stems down until they are bent over completely and snap.

You will want to grow the following pennisetums for their fountains of fluffy plumes. They are happiest on well-drained sunny sites, and are frost hardy. On *P. alopecuroides*, the ordinary linear dark green leaves grow to about 60cm/2ft long. Of the same size and spread, *P. villosum* is a most graceful and appealing grass: also known as 'feathertop', it has white plumes that look like stretched bunny tails. In cold climates its seed is not viable, but in warm climates it self-seeds prolifically – and you may wish to avoid it because of this. Pennisetums are summer- and autumn-flowering, and the plumes on this one can be as tall as 1.5m/5ft. *P. macrourum* has evergreen mid-green leaves to 60cm/2ft in length with long-bristled spikelets that begin pale green, maturing to pale brown and purple. The overall height is 1.8m/6ft with a spread up to 1.2m/4ft.

Molinia caerulea subsp. *arundinacea* prefers acidic conditions, moist and well-drained conditions too. Molinias will take some shade and are fully hardy. 'Karl Foerster' has leaves about 80cm/32in long, with open panicles of purple spikelets on arching stems which leap out to a startling 2m/7ft. As with *Stipa gigantea*, the airy spikelets lend themselves to being looked through.

Swords of yucca form the backbone planting between red plumes of *Anemanthele lessoniana* (syn. *Stipa arundinacea*) with spiky *Furcraea selloa*, orange *Canna indica* 'Purpurea' and yellow *Rudbeckia fulgida* 'Goldsturm' to the rear. Purple *Lavandula stoechas* (foreground) makes a low dome among the frothy fountains.

GREY-LEAVED GRASSES

Like most grey-leaved plants, glaucous grasses like full sun and well-drained soil that is not especially rich.

Hardy *Helictotrichon sempervirens* makes a neat spray of grey-blue leaves 23cm/9in long. Unlike many grasses this one shows its spikelets in early to midsummer, turning straw-coloured and lasting well as the season progresses. The plumes will reach almost 1.5m/5ft on a mature specimen. This evergreen grass needs to be planted in a group to make its presence felt.

Festuca glauca is smaller, 20cm/8in tall, and a good reliable evergreen grass, again flowering early in the summer with blue-green flowers 30cm/12in tall. To retain its colour it has to be divided every three years or so. It bulks up quite fast and is fully hardy.

You have to be careful to pick the right elymus for the job. Elymus are fully hardy wild rye grasses, some so vigorous that they are used for stabilizing dunes. You may not be rapturous about them if your garden becomes infested with an invasive variety and stiff leaves with sharp tips can be lethal; but the intense blue of the following grasses makes it hard not to fall under their spell.

Elytrigia repens (syn. *Elymus repens*), common couch grass, is best avoided in a garden setting, unless you are aiming to colonize a wild area. *Elymus magellanicus* has electric-blue leaves 15cm/12in long. *E. hispidus* flowers early in the summer with silvery sky-blue leaves up to 20cm/8in long. The foliage is the main attraction; the flowers are insignificant. All are fully hardy.

Species of holcus are also inclined to be over-vigorous. It is best to stick to the attractive and well-behaved *H. mollis* 'Albovariegatus'. Bear in mind that generally it cannot stand full sun and poor soil which may dry out totally, although it is fine in full sun in northern England, Scotland and Northern Ireland. Try it in a moist, open, well-drained area and it will be fine. It is also useful in partial shade and is fully hardy. Once the new deciduous shoots have settled down, *H. mollis* 'Albovariegatus' often has the look of having just been sat on. It forms a prostrate mat, with a few leaves sticking up, as if it needed a quick haircut. When you look down on it, it looks like spiky shards of frost. Although they look hard, the green leaves are soft, dominated by wide white margins. Growing to about 45cm/18in long, it has pale green spikelets up to 12cm/5in tall. You should not find this one too vigorous, but avoid partnering it with neighbours of a less colonizing instinct.

ABOVE, TOP *Helictotrichon sempervirens* **ABOVE, BOTTOM** *Holcus mollis* 'Variegatus' **OPPOSITE** In Sydney, New South Wales, flames of sansevieria foliage in the foreground frame a simple design of *Agave attenuata* and *Festuca glauca*. Note the raised bed.

ACHIEVING CONTRASTS

Grasses can be a problem to gardeners. Easily dominated by brasher neighbours, they are sometimes herded together, perhaps on the safety-in-numbers principle. Worse still, one might be planted as a specimen, as a token nod to the fact that at least one grass should be included in a garden setting. Some front gardens seem to excel at this style, with a lone, giant pampas grass, *Cortaderia selloana*, in pride of place. But neither planting style does a lot for grasses. They make such superb foils that they are often best integrated with other plants to vary the pace: they set each other off. It is no use having one grass on its own, unrelated to its neighbours.

Grasses can also look too uniform on their own. Their similarity of leaf shape and habit, as in sticking up straight, or emerging as fountains with arching leaves, means that they often need breaking up with other plants to maintain interest. A border concentrating solely on grasses either looks municipal or too redolent of a botanic garden. They look better when complemented by different flowers or shapes, and their delicate flowers and fluffy seedheads create contrasting fountains with barbs and spikes, or with spiky swords and lances, with whom they make admirable bedfellows. Indeed as the unyielding swords cry out for some soft delicacy.

If planted solely in a border, grasses need to be self-supporting to look good. Think how dashed down tall, neglected lawn grass becomes: by midsummer it usually looks as if the cat or the dog have indulged in endless siestas there, with flattened pockets among what is left standing. This can be true of grasses in the border.

You can experiment with grasses in various ways. The recent fascination with prairie planting, developed in the 1990s, came to their rescue. You can follow this style by creating a low-maintenance scheme with robust undemanding perennials and self-supporting grasses. This naturalistic look has often been promoted on a large scale – in municipal plantings and individuals' private gardens on generous sites. If you are not quite sure how to place grasses successfully, coupling them with low-maintenance perennials offers an obvious juxtaposition of shapes. Because most grasses tend to look at their best from midsummer to late autumn, late-performing perennials such as cone flowers (*Rudbeckia*) make appropriate companions. Rudbeckias are excellent: the open daisy flowers are not too sophisticated for the simple ribbon shapes of grasses and the brown flower cone harmonizes with their autumnal mood.

However, it can be hard to make a convincing prairie-style planting scheme within the limitations of a small domestic setting; after all, prairies signify infinite space and huge skies. But prairie-style planting with grasses and perennials can be adapted in a small garden. Within the parameters of sharp gardening, you can shift the emphasis from planting grasses with late-flowering perennials and dream up heady combinations with thistly or globe flowers, interspersed with sabre-like swords. Focus on the globe flowers of agapanthus or alliums to create explosions among grasses. Inspire with spiky eryngium and echinops flowers to contrast with their featheriness.

You can also achieve contrasts by placing plants of different heights or foliage colour alongside each other, or by contrasting flowering spikes, seedheads and foliage form.

Having said that, I maintain that grasses are often seen to best advantage with stronger neighbours. A sea of grasses, even if it combines grasses of several different shapes and sizes, may still lack a focal point. This is where sharp gardening comes in. By allowing some spears to glimmer among them you create a stronger image.

The contemporary planting style (see page 146) which reverses the normal time-honoured method of placing smaller plants at the front, grading them gradually to the tallest specimens at the back of the border – no one bats an eyelid if taller plants are placed at the front of a border. After all, plants with an open, almost transparent form, are seen to better advantage in the foreground – is easily achievable with taller grasses of an open habit.

The flowering spike of an agave catches the sun at Carol Valentine's garden in Montecito, California.

Contemporary style using grasses among spikes

Carol Valentine's garden in Montecito, California, is an arrangement of amber-painted concrete terraces spreading out below her angular white stucco home. Its rectilinear architecture – the house was designed in 1983 and with its flat roofs and high vertical walls looks as though it has been carved out of blocks – creates various hard lean lines which act as a platform for the sharp planting below. Spiky plants and grasses are as one with the architecture and summer droughts here. In the full glare of the Californian sun both the angular shapes of the house and the spiny silhouettes create startling shadows. The spikes echo the crisp lines and the fluffy sprays of ornamental grasses inject a welcome softness and delicacy. Because there is virtually no rainfall between spring and autumn, and mains water is rationed, garden designer Isabelle Greene chose drought-tolerant plants such as aloes and agaves and the native *Yucca whipplei*, which shrug off the harsh conditions. Cushions of echeverias hug the ground, and fountains of grasses add an inspired relief to the stark silhouettes of the yuccas and agaves.

Below the garden the ground descends into the native evergreen oak woodland, but above this there is a panoramic view of the Pacific Ocean and the Santa Barbara Channel. As well as this backdrop the design of the garden and its terraces were inspired by an aerial view of Balinese rice paddies. It would have been easy to have made the terraces as angular as the house. The amber concrete retaining walls echo the white stucco of the house, forming different-sized planting pockets and beds as they wander haphazardly across the gently sloping site. To inject softness the corners of the various terraces are often rounded. Poured concrete is enhanced with a bit of texture, so each wall was created between lengths of split cedar to introduce waves and irregularities.

The rugged planting keeps to a minimalist vein, and the effect is starkly beautiful. Its simplicity, and its appropriateness for the climate, view and house, make it a uniquely satisfying image. The waving octopus-like tendrils of the aloes, agaves seeming to float like giant water-lily flowers among fountains of grasses, and ground-hugging echeverias like sea urchins inject the garden with a marine quality.

ABOVE *Echeveria* 'Cameo'. **RIGHT** Tufts of grasses such as this pennisetum explode like sea spray among the strangely marine-like aloes, yuccas and agaves on Carol Valentine's terraces.

Grasses and spikes

In my first seaside garden in Grange-over-Sands, Cumbria, with an ample rainfall of 107cm/43in per annum, I modified this crisp modern Californian planting style when designing a steeply terraced limestone rockery. This comprises four terraces about 75cm/30in wide, each 6m/20ft long, supported by rockery stones.

I wanted to create an exotic-looking garden here, but I had to do it with frost-hardy plants, as frost-tender plants such as aloes and agaves, which would have looked perfect, can only be overwintered inside in a climate of winter wet and occasional frosts, so were out of the question. Instead I created a desert theme by planting a dozen or so yellow-margined *Yucca gloriosa* 'Variegata' as the main theme plant. These yuccas seem impervious to winter wet, and will eventually form 1m/39in trunks in England. Variephobes might blanch at the thought of so many variegated plants in one setting but, perversely, a concentration of variegated plants makes them look 'normal': you forget their eyecatching stripes and concentrate on the shapes, which unify the design. After three years, they are roughly a uniform size, and the variegations all match with no reversions. One or two of the plants have made two crowns, but this does not detract from the effect. I call it 'poor man's California'.

Repeated plantings of the evergreen *Fascicularia bicolor* continue the theme. These low, sprawling porcupine-like plants are curiosities. They could never be described as pretty but in late summer and autumn the sizzling red central rosettes are eyecatching.

Barbed *Dasylirion acrotrichum*, resembling a fibre-optic lamp, takes centre-stage. All these plants provide evergreen structure.

To inject variety and movement I punctuated the spikes with drifts of grasses. The ones that look most content and appropriate are the stipas, which after three seasons are roughly the same height as the yuccas at 30cm/12in. *Anemanthele lessoniana* turns orange-brown in winter; bleached golden *Stipa tenuissima*, planted on the edge of the path, is such a tactile plant and the fineness of the leaves makes for the ultimate contrast with sword-like foliage. The fine leaves of *Deschampsia cespitosa* continue the theme. *Stipa gigantea*'s transparent plumes are easily looked through, so I have placed them on the second lowest tier, which creates perspective. At the top of the rockery, in the area most exposed to sea winds, the sturdy plumes of *Cortaderia richardii* never topple. They last indefinitely, the plumes gradually fraying to nothing, while the stems remain impervious to winter gales. Surrounded by grasses, the stark shapes of the spiky plants, stacked above each other, make unforgettable silhouettes. I had not expected that the grasses would look at their best during winter. Even though they are a supporting cast to the yuccas, they are charismatic in their own right. If frosted in morning sun they seem worth a hundred summer flowers. *Stipa tenuissima*, once again, is the star plant in these conditions, when each single blade is separated and rimed with sugary-sparkly frost.

To add colour to this weaving of textures I

raided my store cupboard of ideas for thistly and globe flowers. On a raised area such as this part of the fun is being able to see the plants at eye level. I packed in several varieties of steely-blue eryngiums, a favourite being *E. planum*, with the yuccas, mostly because I like the flowers, but mainly because they become alive with bees in high summer. You can enjoy them more where you can see them close to on raised beds. I squeezed the eryngiums underneath the rockery stones – not as root protection, but to tuck them away in the hope that they would not grow too vigorously and swamp other plants. As they tend to flop over, and as staking them on a rockery would have looked wildly inappropriate, they look as though they are bursting out from beneath the rocks, and have self-seeded there. The fact that their skeletal bracts cling on for much of winter means that they are virtually a twelve-month perennial. The alliums are randomly dotted in groups of five or more. *A. cristophii*, with its big bold heads, has the right proportions for growing with the dagger-like yucca foliage. *A. schubertii* has larger heads on shorter stems, so to make impact should be planted on a raised bed; it is lost in a border at ground level, and who wants to bend down that far to admire them?

For underplanting and to soften the planting I added low spreading mats of the daisy-flowered *Anthemis punctata* subsp. *cupaniana*. The purple allium flowers look superb above the finely cut silver foliage of the anthemis and the dying allium foliage is soon lost among it. This is an excellent ground-cover perennial for a well-drained sunny spot, especially for a new planting scheme, as it covers 1 square metre/yard in a couple of years.

Transplanting myself to a new garden in Grange-over-Sands in the spring of 2003, I posed myself a *Desert Island Discs* question. The south-east front garden is roughly 10m/30ft square and sloping. Formed into three terraces with the earth retained by 1m/39in limestone walls, it is free-draining and when sunny it does not fall under the shadow of the house until early to late afternoon. I wanted to make this

Verticals of *Acanthus spinosus* and *Cordyline australis* juxtaposed with the flat expanse of Morecambe Bay, Cumbria, in my second garden.

garden more of a seaside-themed garden than the last one. By using grasses I could create the idea of marram grass on sand dunes, and eryngiums would stand in as sea hollies. The evergreen skeleton of the garden would be made up of seaside-loving palms such as *Chamaerops humilis*, cordylines and phormiums.

The question was: if I could have just one grass for the site what would it be? There was not much doubt in my mind. It had to be *Stipa tenuissima*. This time I bought seven rather than three, having learned to simplify in my old age, and paired them with my desert isle phormium, *P. cookianum* subsp. *hookeri* 'Cream Delight'. The blondness of the grass is highlighted by the creamy green-striped phormium leaves. I also planted *Stipa gigantea*, because its plumes appear in early summer, and are transparent and golden. Placed just over 1m/39in from a window, the 2.5m/8ft tall plumes make a graceful, waving screen. Their

airiness cannot hide anything but they act as a first line of defence for the eye to focus on. They also help to create perspective. The eryngiums I have chosen for this area are mainly *E. bourgatii* and *E. giganteum*. I have kept to a restrained palette throughout. For the rosettes I have planted ground-hugging *Fascicularia bicolor* with *Astelia chathamica* 'Silver Spear' next to prostrate rosemary. The predominant plant in a few years will be the dwarf fan palm, *Chamaerops humilis*, of which there are fifteen. Meanwhile three cordylines, which add much-needed height in a new garden, are growing away happily. To add fuzzy-mounded contrast I have used a few Mediterranean subshrubs. I have used two favourite varieties of cistus, the first with matt-textured leaves, the second with glossy foliage: *C.* x *pulverulentus* 'Sunset' because it flowers for most of the summer, and *C. aguilarii* 'Maculatus' for the big dark red blotches at the base of each petal.

LEFT In December the stark evergreen bones of *Yucca gloriosa* 'Variegata' emerge like water-lily flowers amid drifts of *Stipa tenuissima* and *Deschampsia cespitosa* in my first garden overlooking Morecambe Bay. **BELOW** My second garden in Grange-over-Sands, after only twelve months, with *Stipa tenuissima*, phormiums, cordylines and pencil-like *Cupress sempervirens* 'Stricta' (foreground) planted to create perspective.

A blue lawn

ABOVE In Paul Spracklin's garden a river of *Festuca glauca* rests the eye between baby agaves in the foreground and exclamations of cordyline and pseudopanax in the background. **PAGES 186–7** James Fraser's stylized 'Kiwiana' effects: fountains of *Pennisetum macrourum* and *Chionochloa rubra* inject lightness among heavyweights such as *Astelia nervosa* (right), *A. chathamica* 'Silver Spear' and *Trachycarpus wagnerianus* (behind the astelias).

In his garden at South Benfleet, Essex, garden designer Paul Spracklin has created a passing nod to the conventional lawn by sowing an area with the dwarf blue grass, *Festuca glauca*. It looks as though the customary green sward has been given a blue rinse. Appropriately the blue grass picks up the blue-grey foliage of agaves and yuccas in his dry, succulent beds. When he was planning the garden, while recognizing that there was no future for the existing lawn, it occurred to him that he needed the open space it provided, as a rest for the eyes from the surrounding dense planting. He turned the original lawn, below this area, into a pond, encircled by steep, well-drained banks clad in succulents, with jungle-style plants in the lowest levels of the garden.

Paul's 'lawn' picks up on the idea of water as a resting place in the garden. His 'sea' of *Festuca glauca* softens the outline of the hard, spiky succulents and complements their glaucous foliage. It's a perfect match. It's also a great gardening joke. You have already absorbed the fact that this is no ordinary garden, British or not, and realized that there will be no lawn. When you turn the corner and see this audacious gesture, cocking a snook at the previously accepted idea of a lawn as an open space with grass in it, it makes you smile. And of course no mowing is required.

Grasses and spiky New Zealand grasses

In the Brockley (south London) garden of Biddy Bunzl and her partner, garden designer James Fraser, conventional design notions are upturned. New Zealander James's planting reflects his favourite native plants and exotics and uses grasses to complement the spiky specimens.

James has been influenced by the New Zealand landscape, especially the primeval forest in the South Island, and by leading plantsmen and designers such as Piet Oudolf, Beth Chatto, Christopher Lloyd and Angus White of Architectural Plants.

The garden is a rectangular London plot, as wide as the semi-detached Victorian house and roughly twice as long. James has the right conditions for spikes and grasses, as the soil is mostly poor and sandy – heavier in some areas. To get his plantings off to a good start, he imported topsoil and created some raised beds about 30cm/12in deep to improve drainage.

As an introduction to James's style of planting, bizarre effects in the small front garden showcase his ideas. Under the canopy of a high-pruned cherry tree, which dominates much of this area, he has kept to a limited palette of plants – sensible in a small space. Silvery *Astelia chathamica* grows well in the semi-shade, even beneath the tree, and feathery hummocks of tan-coloured *Anemanthele lessoniana*, which are allowed to self-seed, wave between the jagged silhouettes of the astelias. To add height the airy perennial *Verbena bonariensis* provides colour at eye level. Further height is gained with plantings of the unearthly-looking *Pseudopanax ferox*, roughly 2m/7ft high and still growing. These Martian-looking plants, like giant stick insects, make you feel slightly uncomfortable. Roughly cut up-ended pieces of reclaimed planking marking the boundary are similarly disarming.

All this slightly prepares you for the back garden, where the theme explodes. Torn planks, 2m/7ft high, looking like a wall of jagged teeth, are left stark. Climbers would clutter the design. The randomly cut planks of elm, iroko and oak, reclaimed from the London docks, and aged railway sleepers make this 1998 garden look older than it is. They are a good way of making hard landscaping look natural. French railway sleepers are preferable to English, as they have not been smothered in creosote and do not poison nearby plants. These sleepers are also used as steps, back-filled with gravel. The same worn timbers are used as decking next to the house, and as raised walkways which lead you down to the furthest end of the garden. The design is totally assymetrical.

There are three paths leading down to the furthest end. Although the soil is not damp, James achieves a feeling of boggy ground by introducing duckboards traversing what is apparently a swamp, supported by randomly spaced reclaimed elm jetty posts. This duckboarding floats above generous blocks of grasses, such as *Calamagrostis brachytricha* and molinia. It also creates a change of level – useful in a flat garden. James regards grasses as being made to be wandered through. Other grasses include *Miscanthus sinensis* 'Silberspinne', housed in a pot which James admits is not ideal

if continued for too many years as it needs moisture. He also chose *Chionochloa rubra*, from New Zealand, because it flowers from mid to late summer.

James's planting follows the lead of his hard landscaping. He has created distinct areas – a dry bed, a moist area and a patch of prairie-style planting – as well as a vegetable garden. He favours a 'naturalistic' use of fluffy, tactile grasses juxtaposed with spiky *Trachycarpus fortunei*, cordylines, astelias, phormiums and a succulent bed of agaves and echeverias. He even has the tender *Yucca elephantipes*, usually sold as a houseplant, growing tall and healthy.

James finds New Zealand evergreens well suited for the kind of structural planting he requires for his designs and over 75 per cent of the plants in his schemes are New Zealand natives. His starting point for any design is incorporating height and texture. Architectural evergreens such as cordylines and pseudo-panax are used to create the structure. He then infills with what he calls mid-range architectural plants such as astelias and phormiums. Once this evergreen backbone is in place he adds deciduous plants – biennials, annuals, perennials and grasses. He favours umbellifers because they provide tall species that rise above the fray.

James emphasizes that it is vital to get the balance right. The evergreen structural planting must be meaty enough to anchor everything else, but not so much as to create maintenance problems down the line. This is why the small trees such as pseudopanax are perfect, as they are so slender. Underplanted with broader-leaved clumps of astelia, they make a dramatic combination, highly prized in winter. Then, by planting feathery grasses such as *Chionochloa rubra*, *Pennisetum macrourum* and *Anemanthele lessoniana*, all tough enough to withstand partial shade, he has made sure that the lower storey plants will not suffer when shade becomes more dominant. As the last two grasses are self-seeders their survival is ensured, and self-seeding makes the planting scheme more informal. He has found that spiky-flowered perennials such as the cardoon thistle, *Cynara cardunculus*, and *Cirsium rivulare* are easily divided, resettling well, so he repeats them to complete the spiky picture.

Although James's style of gardening is contemporary, his maintenance priorities are time-honoured. He insists on mulching. James and Biddy find that the results give pleasure all year round while being low maintenance and informal. This, surely, is the essence of sharp gardening.

Spangled stems of *Chionochloa rubra* sprinkled over the boardwalk contrast with the severe shapes of *Agave attenuata* in pots with pebbles from Lake Taupo in New Zealand. Brittle and skeletal, *Pseudopanax ferox* (centre back) and *P. crassifolius* (right back) make a foil for the chunky cacti-like *Euphorbia pseudocactus*, overwintered indoors.

Index

Page numbers in *italic* refer to the captions to illustrations

AUTHOR'S ACKNOWLEDGMENTS Thank you to my parents, Una and Peter Holliday, who started me off mowing, clipping and weeding from an early age and sowed the seeds for my love of plants and gardening, and dread of lawns! I am eternally grateful to Erica Hunningher, who provided the title, and without whose support *Sharp Gardening* might never have got off the ground. To create a book using commissioned photographs from a renowned photographer is a luxury. Jerry Harpur's pictures breathe life into the theme in a way I could only have dreamed of. I shall miss Jerry's frantic telephone calls when on location and rapturous exclamations when the light was kind. Frances Lincoln offered a fine support team to whom I am indebted. Both Anne Fraser and Jo Christian, consistently upbeat and positive, have made our meetings fruitful and fun. Anne Askwith has been an inspirational editor, making splendid suggestions in the final stages. Caroline Clark, the designer, has matched Jerry's photographs to the text imaginatively and beautifully. Tony Lord has eradicated any howlers in the plant names. I would like to thank all the garden owners and designers mentioned; Nicholas Henshall who inspired me to write in the first place; Paul Evans who kept me laughing in the difficult periods; and Robert Gaby in Toronto, who engendered optimism. My final thanks to David Parker, who finished our garden while I completed the book; ever-faithful Toby, who has been with me in both my gardens; and to Freddie, who arrived the day my text was delivered to the publishers.

Over the years I have found the following helpful: Myles Challis, *Exotic Gardening in Cool Climates*, 1986 (paperback edition Fourth Estate, 1994); Beth Chatto, *The Dry Garden*, Weidenfeld and Nicolson, 1981; *Beth Chatto's Gravel Garden*, Frances Lincoln, 2000; Mary and Gary Irish, *Agaves, Yuccas, and Related Plants*, Timber Press, 2000; and Charles Quest-Ritson, *The English Gardener Abroad*, Viking, 1992.

PHOTOGRAPHIC ACKNOWLEDGMENTS
a = above, b = below, c = centre, l = left, r = right

PHOTOGRAPHS © JERRY HARPUR
2–3 Great Dixter, Northiam, Sussex; 6 garden in Montecito, California, designed by the Harris brothers; 9 Carol Valentine, Montecito, California, designed by Isabelle C. Greene, Santa Barbara, California; 10 Abbey Gardens, Tresco; 13 Peter Causer and Roja Dove, Brighton, Sussex; 14a Mexico University Botanic Garden; 14b Geelong Botanic Garden, Victoria, Australia; 16 the Kotoske garden, designed by Steve Martino, Phoenix, Arizona; 19 Silas Mountsier's garden, New Jersey, designed by Richard Hartlage; 20 Abbey Gardens, Tresco; 21 designed by Davis Dalbok, San Francisco; 23 Abbey Gardens, Tresco; 24 Beth Chatto, Elmstead Market, Essex; 25 Beth Chatto, Elmstead Market, Essex; 26 Marie Harley, Stockwell, south London; 28 Thomas Hobbs and Brent Elliott, Vancouver; 31 the Montefiore garden, designed by Raymond Jungles, Miami; 33 Peter Causer and Roja Dove, Brighton, Sussex; 34r Charney Well, Grange-over-Sands, Cumbria, designed by Christopher Holliday; 35a RHS Wisley, Surrey; 35b designed by Richard Hartlage, Seattle; 36l Charney Well, Grange-over-Sands, Cumbria, designed by Christopher Holliday; 38 Mr and Mrs I.B. Kathuria, Maida Vale, London; 39a Charney Well, Grange-over-Sands, Cumbria, designed by Christopher Holliday; 39b Abbey Gardens, Tresco, 40–41 Chateau de Vauville, Normandy; 43 Dennis Schrader and Bill Smith, Mattituck, Long Island, New York; 44 RHS Hyde Hall, Essex; 45 Lady Walton's garden: La Mortella, Ischia; 46r designed by Richard Hartlage for Graeme Hardie, New Jersey; 47a Villa Ramsdal, Chelmsford, Essex; 47c Wave Hill, The Bronx, New York; 47b RHS Hyde Hall, Essex; 48 Thomas Hobbs and Brent Beattie, Vancouver; 50l designed by Eric Nagelman for Kent Damon, Montecito, California; 50–51 Sue Nathan, Bonython Manor, Helston, Cornwall; 51 Beth Chatto, Elmstead Market, Essex; 52bl Sue Nathan, Bonython Manor, Helston, Cornwall; 52br designed by Bunny Guinness for Stonemarket, RHS Chelsea 2004; 53a Wave Hill, The Bronx, New York; 53b Titoke Point, Taihape, New Zealand; 55l Villa Ramsdal, Chelmsford, Essex; 55r Helen Dillon, Ranelagh, Dublin; 57 Abbotsbury Gardens, Dorset; 58 Abbotsbury Gardens, Dorset; 59 Abbotsbury Gardens, Dorset; 62 RHS Hyde Hall, Essex; 63 Lamorran House, Cornwall; 64 Charney Well, Grange-over-Sands, Cumbria, designed by Christopher Holliday; 65l The Old Vicarage, East Ruston, Norfolk, 66 the Kotoske garden, designed by Steve Martino, Phoenix, Arizona; 68–9 Huntington Botanic Garden, San Marino, California; 73 Beverley McConnell, Ayrlies, Auckland, New Zealand; 74–5, Beverley McConnell, Ayrlies, Auckland, New Zealand; 76 Geelong Botanic Garden, Victoria, Australia; 78 Ruth Bancroft Garden, Walnut Creek, California; 80al Ruth Bancroft Garden, Walnut Creek, California; 80ar Carol Valentine's garden, Montecito, California; 80bl Geelong Botanic Garden, Victoria, Australia; 80br designed by Bernard Hickie, Dublin; 81 Mexico University Botanic Garden; 83 designed by Philip Nash at RHS Chelsea, 2004; 84–5 Mexico University Botanic Garden; 86 Charney Well, Grange-over-Sands, Cumbria, designed by Christopher Holliday; 87a Mr and Mrs I.B. Kathuria, Maida Vale, London; 87b Geelong Botanic Garden, Victoria, Australia; 88 Beth Chatto, Elmstead Market, Essex; 89 Jardin du Luxembourg, Paris; 90al Helen Dillon, Ranelagh, Dublin; 90ar Abbey Gardens, Tresco; 90b Huntington Botanic Garden, San Marino, California; 91 Beverley McConnell, Ayrlies, Auckland, New Zealand; 92a Huntington Botanic Garden, San Marino, California; 92b Beverley McConnell, Ayrlies, Auckland, New Zealand; 93 Mexico University Botanic Garden; 94 RHS Hyde Hall, Essex; 95l designed by Andrea Cochran, San Francisco; 95r designed by Isabelle C. Greene, Santa Barbara, California; 96–7 Abbey Gardens, Tresco; 98 Huntington Botanic Garden, San Marino, California; 99 Yewbarrow House, Grange-over-Sands, Cumbria, designed by Christopher Holliday; 100 Helen Dillon, Ranelagh, Dublin; 103 designed by Bernard Hickie, Dublin and Declan Buckley, London; 104 designed by Bernard Hickie, Dublin, and Declan Buckley, London; 105 Bernard Hickie's garden, Dublin; 108–9 designed by Jason Payne for Chester Marsh, Sydenham, London; 110–11 Declan Buckley's garden, London; 113 designed by Richard Hartlage, Seattle; 114 Ruth Bancroft, Walnut Creek, California; 115 Mexico University Botanic Garden; 116 Helen Dillon, Ranelagh, Dublin; 118 Geelong Botanic Garden, Victoria, Australia; 121a Nori and Sandra Pope, Hadspen House, Somerset; 122–3 RHS Hyde Hall, Essex; 124 Yewbarrow House, Grange-over-Sands, Cumbria, designed by Christopher Holliday; 125 RHS Wisley, Surrey; 126a RHS Wisley, Surrey; 126c Linda Cochran, Bainbridge Island, Nr. Seattle; 127 RHS Hyde Hall, Essex; 128 Beth Chatto, Elmstead Market, Essex; 128–9 Christopher Holliday's garden, Grange-over-Sands, Cumbria; 130 Huntington Botanic Garden, San Marino, California; 130–31 Beverley McConnell, Ayrlies, Auckland, New Zealand; 131 Villa Ramsdal, Chelmsford, Essex; 133 Logan Botanic Garden, Stranraer, Scotland; 134 La Casella, Opio, Nr. Grasse, France; 135 RHS Hyde Hall, Essex; 136 RHS Hyde Hall, Essex; 137a Biddy Bunzl's garden, Brockley, south London, designed by James Fraser, Avant Gardener, London; 137b Eltham Palace, London; 139a Jill Cowley, Park Farm, Essex; 139b Beth Chatto, Elmstead Market, Essex; 140 Jardin des Paradis, Cordes, France, designed by Eric Ossart and Arnaud Maurieres; 141 Merrill Lynch garden, RHS Chelsea 2004, designed by Dan Pearson; 143 National Trust, Anglesey Abbey, Cambridge; 145 Leeds Castle, Kent; 147 the Kotoske garden, designed by Steve Martino, Phoenix, Arizona; 148 the Binns garden, designed by Christy ten Eyck, Phoenix, Arizona; 149 the Kotoske garden, designed by Steve Martino, Phoenix, Arizona; 150 Yewbarrow House, Grange-over-Sands, Cumbria, designed by Christopher Holliday; 152–3 RHS Hyde Hall, Essex; 155 the Bauer Garden, designed by Mary Effron and Javier Valdivia, Santa Monica, California; 156 Yewbarrow House, Grange-over-Sands, Cumbria, designed by Christopher Holliday; 158–9 Yewbarrow House, Grange-over-Sands, Cumbria, designed by Christopher Holliday; 160 RHS Wisley, Surrey; 163 Wave Hill, The Bronx, New York; 165a Glen Chantry, Wickham Bishops, Essex; 165b RHS Hyde Hall, Essex; 167al RHS Wisley, Surrey; 167ar Biddy Bunzl's garden, Brockley, south London, designed by James Fraser, Avant Gardener, London; 167bl Wave Hill, The Bronx, New York; 167br Mexico University Botanic Garden; 169a Adrian Bloom; 169b Glen Chantry, Essex; 169c RHS Hyde Hall, Essex; 170 RHS Wisley, Surrey; 171l Sue Nathan, Bonython Manor, Helston, Cornwall; 171r RHS Hyde Hall, Essex; 173 Sue Nathan, Bonython Manor, Helston, Cornwall; 174b Glen Chantry, Essex; 175 designed by Vladimir Sitta, Sydney, New South Wales; 177 Carol Valentine, Montecito, California, designed by Isabelle C. Greene; 178–9 Carol Valentine, Montecito, California, designed by Isabelle C. Greene; 181 Christopher Holliday's garden, Grange-over-Sands, Cumbria; 182 Charney Well, Grange-over-Sands, Cumbria, designed by Christopher Holliday; 183 Christopher Holliday's garden, Grange-over-Sands, Cumbria; 186–7 Biddy Bunzl's garden, Brockley, south London, designed by James Fraser, Avant Gardener, London; 188 Biddy Bunzl's garden, Brockley, south London, designed by James Fraser, Avant Gardener, London

PHOTOGRAPHS © MARCUS HARPUR
1; 5 Paul Spracklin, Benfleet, Essex; 34l RHS Wisley, Surrey; 34c RHS Wisley, Surrey; 36r RHS Wisley, Surrey; 39c RHS Wisley, Surrey; 52a, 54 RHS Wisley, Surrey; 61 designed by Jason Payne, London, for Phil Gibson; 65r The Old Vicarage, East Ruston, Norfolk; 71 The Old Vicarage, East Ruston, Norfolk; 107 Paul Spracklin, Benfleet, Essex; 121b RHS Hyde Hall, Essex; 126b Beth Chatto, Elmstead Market, Essex; 174a; 184 Paul Spracklin, Benfleet, Essex